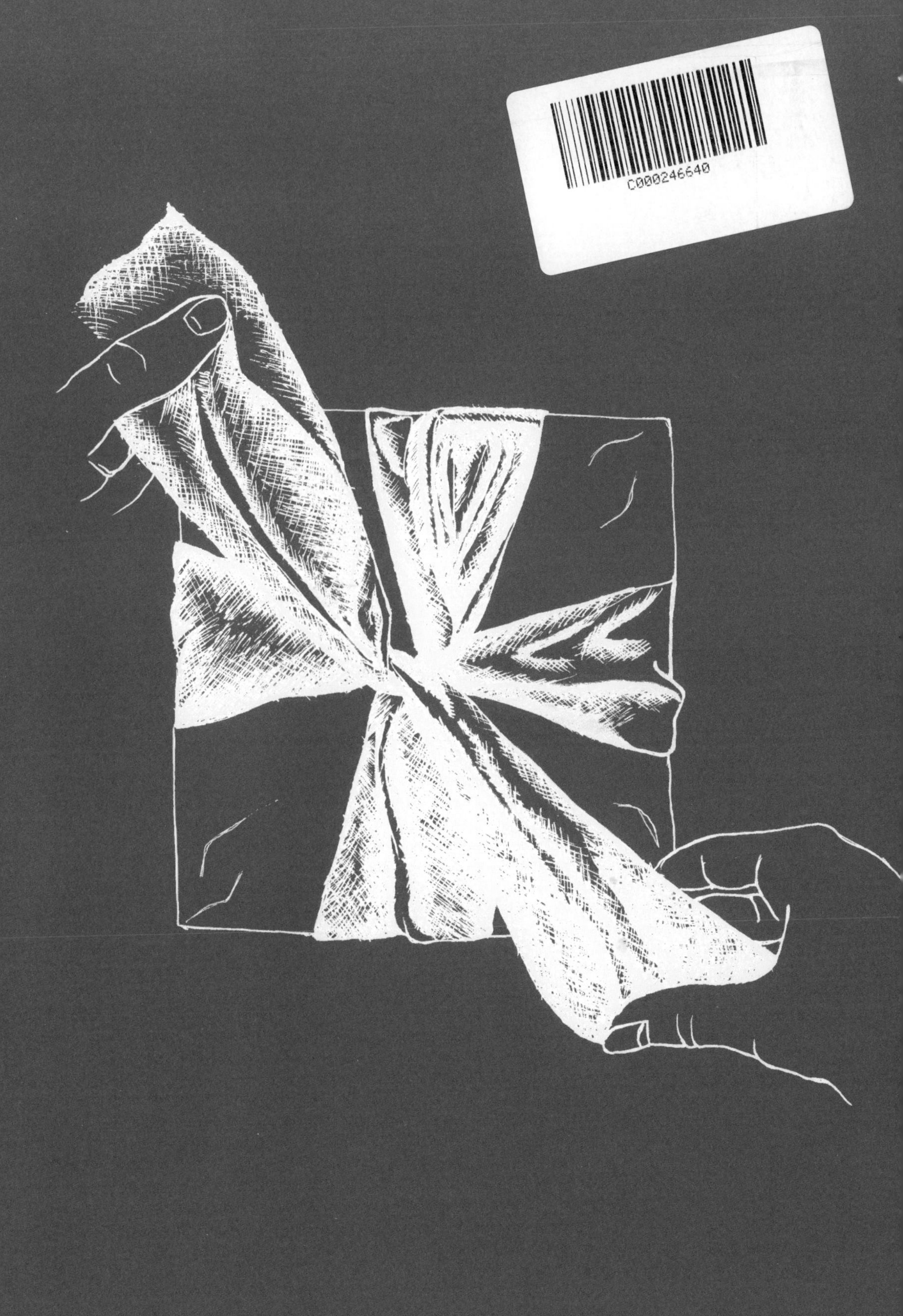

THE

IRISH COUNTRYWOMEN'S ASSOCIATION

BOOK OF CHRISTMAS

Christmas 2016.

For Mam
From Nichola

ABOUT THE ICA

Founded in May 1910, the aim of the Irish Countrywomen's Association (ICA) was 'to improve the standard of life in rural Ireland through education and co-operative effort'. Today the ICA has 518 local Guilds in cities, towns and rural areas throughout Ireland. They continue to offer support and fun as well as opportunities to make friends, learn new skills and contribute to the wider community. Every day, the women share with each other nuggets of advice, tried-and-tested methods and practical help, and they hope this book will pass on some of that knowledge to you. *The ICA Cookbook*, *The ICA Book of Home and Family* and the ICA *Book of Tea and Company* were all bestsellers in Ireland and overseas.

THE IRISH COUNTRYWOMEN'S ASSOCIATION

BOOK OF CHRISTMAS

Recipes, Advice, Blessings and Traditions for the Perfect Irish Christmas

General Editor Aoife Carrigy

GILL BOOKS

GILL BOOKS
Hume Avenue, Park West, Dublin 12
www.gillbooks.ie

Gill Books is an imprint of M.H. Gill & Co.

978 07171 6818 7

General Editor Aoife Carrigy
Index compiled by Eileen O'Neill
Design and print origination by Tanya M Ross, www.elementinc.ie
Illustrations by Tanya M Ross, www.elementinc.ie
Photography © Joanne Murphy, www.joanne-murphy.com
Food stylists: Carly Horan and Blondie Horan. T: 087 922 7662. W: www.styledwithlove.ie
Food cooked and baked by Carly Horan and Blondie Horan
Assistant to chefs and stylists: Katie Tsouros
Printed by BZ Graf. S.A. Poland

PROPS SUPPLIED BY
Ashley Cottage Interiors, Ballyard, Tralee, Co. Kerry. T: 087 922 7662. W: www.styledwithlove.ie
Historic Interiors, Oberstown, Lusk, Co. Dublin. T: 01 843 7174
Meadows & Byrne, Dun Laoghaire, Co. Dublin. T: 01 280 4554. W: www.meadowsandbyrne.com

This book is typeset in Lora 8.5pt on 12pt and Verlag 10pt on 12pt.

The paper used in this book comes from the wood pulp of managed forests.
For every tree felled, at least one tree is planted, thereby renewing natural resources.

A CIP catalogue record for this book is available from the British Library.

5 4 3

LOVE

Contents

Introduction

I am delighted to introduce *The Irish Countrywomen's Association Book of Christmas*. This is the fourth in this series of books written collectively by our members, each of which has focused on a particular area of ICA expertise and experience. In *The ICA Cookbook*, we shared favourite recipes that had sustained and brought pleasure to our families down through the generations. *The ICA Book of Home and Family* gathered our considerable stock of practical wisdom and various skills called upon in running a busy household. And, most recently, *The ICA Book of Tea and Company* was a reflective book that combined the art of teatime hospitality with some treasured words of wisdom that have brought sustenance to our hearts and souls over the years.

We are proud of what these three books represent in terms of the breadth of our shared experience. But we felt there was one other area in which ICA women excel, and that is the preparation of a special family Christmas and all the traditional food, celebratory decorations and craft-based homemade gifts that come with it. This is a very creative time of year during which ICA members take great pleasure in showcasing and utilising their varied skills and practical knowledge. We share those skills – and that pleasure – in these pages.

For ICA women, Christmas is so much more than just a day or even a week: it is a season. It is a busy time, one associated with many traditional and ritualistic deeds: mixing the cake, lighting the Christmas candle, giving presents to loved ones. And it is a time when we give thanks for the work of our friends and colleagues throughout the year. It is the season when we cherish our families, children and grandchildren, and celebrate the Christian traditions of our land.

It is also a time associated with words: with seasonal blessings, with folklore and with the retelling of the story that is at the heart of this Christian holiday, that of a birth in a manger. There are many more stories worth retelling too, of Christmases past and their important lessons about life and love. Each of us has treasured memories of Christmas: often sentimental, sometimes poignant but also joyful. Many of these have been gathered in these pages, alongside much-loved traditions from ICA families and their localities. All Irish families have their own Christmas traditions – I know we certainly do in my family. These traditions are what we hand down to the next generation and they will be how our grandchildren remember Christmas.

We hope that this *ICA Book of Christmas* will provide you with a little bit of help and ICA know-how to help create a convivial Christmas for you and your family. We hope too that it might keep you busy making beautiful decorations and gifts in the run-up to the festive season; entice you to make some tasty Christmas treats that you may not have tried before and bring a little light into the dark days of winter as you read the poems, excerpts from Irish authors and family stories.

Nollaig Shona Daoibh.

In Friendship,

Marie O'Toole, *National President of the Irish Countrywomen's Association*

A NOTE FROM THE EDITOR, AOIFE CARRIGY

Christmas is a very special time for families, and an Irish Christmas is particularly special. It's a time of tradition and of celebration, of social and family gatherings and homecomings. It is both a time to step out of our busy daily lives and reflect on the world we live in, and a whirlwind of eating, drinking, making merry and reminding those around us that we care for them through the gifts we share with them. And who better than the women of the Irish Countrywomen's Association to guide us through this special season, with their wealth of practical experience and their store of precious festive memories?

As with *The ICA Cookbook*, this *ICA Book of Christmas* sees these women share recipes from their kitchens with you. Some have been passed down faithfully through generations, others picked up and perfected along the way. In several cases we have included more than one version of Christmas essentials. Just as there is no definitive brown soda bread, there is no definitive Christmas cake or plum pudding recipe. Instead there are many that work very well for the families who have tried and tested them over years of enjoyment. Each of the recipes shared here offers something a little different.

Christmas can bring out the best in us – but it can also be a minefield of planning and co-ordinating. As with *The ICA Book of Home and Family*, here you will find practical advice for an easier life, with secret shortcuts and tips on everything from getting the house shipshape to cooking up a festive feast to producing homemade Christmas crafts and gifts.

And like *The ICA Book of Tea and Company*, this unique book gathers much-loved lines from poems, short stories and carols, placing them alongside blessings, customs and traditions from Christmases past. What makes this book extra special is its store of first-hand recollections of an Ireland of another time, one where women like Sheila O'Connor would bake her Christmas bread over an open fire with a hot sod of turf placed on the oven lid. That traditional turf-fuelled oven may have been replaced with a modern kitchen in most Irish homes, but Sheila's Christmas bread is still being baked every year by her granddaughter in Dublin and her great-grandchildren from Antrim to Vancouver. Ireland may have changed, but we have taken our past with us on that journey, and it's at times like Christmas that this becomes most evident.

In collating each of these books it has struck me time and again just how much of an island nation we are. One where community is hugely important, where neighbours are often an extension of the extended family, but also one greatly influenced by the world beyond its shores. And so, alongside recipes that have travelled the world from a turf-fuelled hearth in County Kerry, we also have recipes that have come the other way: Thanksgiving recipes for harvest vegetables picked up during decades of emigration, Goan-style Christmas cake fragrant with Spice Route aromas of an exotic childhood, Portuguese kings' cake brought to an adopted home from sunnier climes.

To spend time with *The ICA Book of Christmas* is to get an insight into an Ireland of yesterday, of today and of tomorrow – and to discover many surprises among the enduring traditions that we Irish know and love. We hope this book helps you to get the most out of this very special season, from the preparations to the gatherings to the great unwinding at the heart of the season.

Chapter 1

Christmas is Coming:

A Time to Prepare

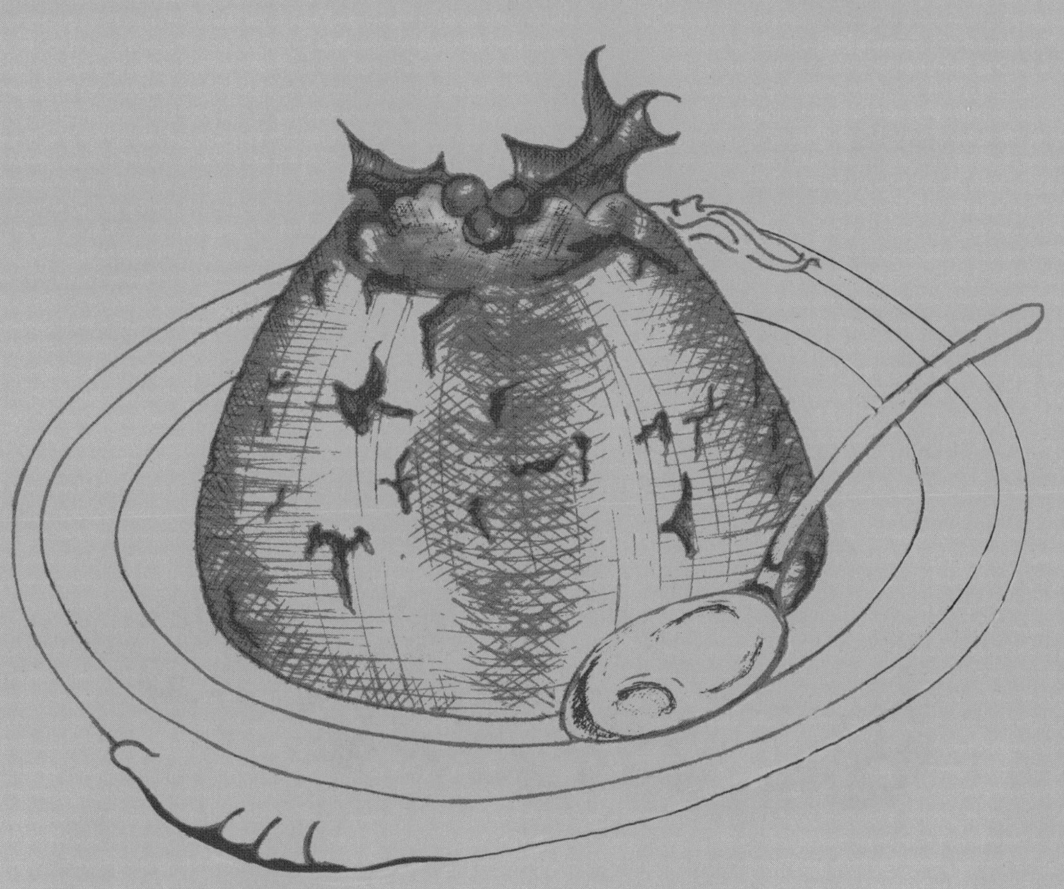

EIRE
EIRE 68c

Sweet Anticipation

Can there be a more nostalgic and evocative ritual than mixing the seasonal fruit for the steamed plum pudding and baked Christmas cake? In the days before the convenience of food processors for blitzing breadcrumbs, and pre-prepared packets of fruit and nuts available all year around, this annual task was quite the event. Raisins had to be stoned by hand, huge pieces of candied peel chopped up into manageable pieces, stale bread grated and almonds blanched, peeled and chopped.

Children would be drafted in to help, and maybe get a lick of the spoon if they were lucky. And for good luck, tradition demands that when the Christmas pudding is being mixed everyone in the house should take a turn and make a wish. Of course, you could buy your cake and pudding every year instead – but, sure, where would be the fun in that?

"November and December is such a lovely time, bringing autumn colours and preparations for Christmas. I usually start my own preparations by making two Christmas puddings. In line with my family tradition, it would be unusual to make just one pudding for your own family! We make puddings for other family members too. I always steam my puddings on the cooker top, and the smell always brings me right back to my childhood.

My Granny wouldn't make any arrangements to make the puddings until muscatel raisins arrived in Dublin. On her twice weekly shopping trip, she would enquire in Findlaters in Thomas Street as to when the muscatels were expected. When they were finally available she would then make a special trip in to Findlaters to get the required amount of raisins. Batch loaf bread was collected from the bakers and left to go stale in the parlour. When I saw the bread going stale, I knew the day was approaching for the great Christmas pudding bake.

The big tin bath, no longer used for anything other than washing clothes, was brought in from the shed and scrubbed in preparation for the mixing. All the ingredients would be assembled and the bread grated into the mixture (no food processor to make breadcrumbs then!). The raisins had to be stoned, and all the fruit washed thoroughly and allowed to dry for a couple of days. There was a lot of preparation before everything was ready for mixing.

Once the puddings had been mixed, steamed and rewrapped, they were ready to be dispatched. One pudding was sent to my uncle in Bedfordshire, another to my aunt in Birmingham. One was sent to old friends of my Granny in Enniskerry, and one to old friends in Edenderry (who, by the way, sent an oven-ready goose to my Granddad on the train from Edenderry to Heuston Station). Plus a couple of puddings for our house and a couple for my Granny. So a lot of puddings to make, steam and store!"

– Marian Cole, Drogheda Guild, Louth

ICA Tip

Tie a double band of brown paper around the outside of the tin to stop the cake from drying out in the oven, as per the Goan Christmas Cake page 7

Knockranna Christmas Cake

CLAIRE ANN MCDONNELL, MONEYSTOWN GUILD, WICKLOW

This old recipe, taken from my mother's book and passed down from her mother, is the Christmas cake I remember eating as a child growing up in Knockranna, one of the highest villages in Ireland. It should be made at the beginning of November, and goes down a treat every year at our Guild's Christmas meeting.

Makes a 23cm (9in) square cake

- 225g (8oz) raisins
- 225g (8oz) currants
- 225g (8oz) sultanas
- 140g (5oz) mixed peel
- 140g (5oz) glacé cherries
- 140g (5oz) ground almonds
- 1 lemon, grated zest and juice
- 1 orange, grated zest and juice
- 30ml (1fl oz) whiskey (about half a small glass), plus an extra 2 tablespoons
- 225g (8oz) butter, at room temperature
- 225g (8oz) brown sugar
- 1–2 tablespoons treacle
- 6 medium eggs, room temperature
- 350g (12oz) self-raising flour, sieved
- ½ level teaspoon mixed spice, sieved

To finish

See pages 124–127 for icing and marzipan recipes and ideas

You'll also need

- 23cm (9in) square tin
- brown paper
- greaseproof paper
- tinfoil

1. The night before you make the cake, place all the dried fruit, glacé cherries, ground almonds, grated zest and juice of the lemon and orange in a bowl. Stir in the whiskey and mix well. Cover and leave to steep overnight.

2. The next day, preheat the oven to 170°C/325°F/Gas 3. Line the outside of the tin (sides and bottom) with a layer of good-quality brown paper, which should be about 20cm (8in) in height. You will also need to cut a 25cm (10in) lid for the top. Then line the inside of the tin with a double layer of greaseproof paper the same height as the tin.

3. Cream the butter and sugar well until it is pale and creamy. Stir in the treacle. Add the eggs, one at a time, beating well after each addition. Add the fruit and mix well. Carefully fold in the flour and mixed spice. Turn into the prepared tin and place carefully on the lower or middle shelf of the preheated oven.

4. Bake for 3½ hours in total. After the first hour, reduce the temperature to 150°C/300°F/Gas 2. After another 30 minutes, open the oven and cover the cake, which should now be golden brown, with the brown paper lid. Continue baking but turn the tin in the oven from time to time. After 3 hours, insert a skewer into the centre of the cake: if the skewer comes out clean, the cake is done. If not, bake for up to another 30 minutes, but keep an eye on it as you don't want it to overcook or burn.

5. Once it is cooked, remove from the oven and allow it to cool in the tin. Pour another 2 tablespoons of whiskey over the top of the cake to help preserve it.

6. When it has cooled, wrap the cake in a layer of greaseproof paper and then a layer of foil on the outside. Store in a cool, dry place until Christmas.

Gluten-Free Christmas Cake

MARY MCCARTHY, RATHKEEVAN GUILD, TIPPERARY

This recipe contains no sugar, dairy or wheat, so it makes for a good alternative if feeding family or friends with certain dietary requirements. I picked up the recipe from my daughter, who makes it regularly and has frozen it successfully (given that it doesn't have any alcohol to preserve it).

Makes a 20cm (8in) cake

- 600g (1lb 5oz) mixed dried fruit (raisins, sultanas, currants, prunes, figs, dates)
- 1 teaspoon ground cinnamon
- 1 teaspoon vanilla extract
- l large orange, zest and juice
- 3 tablespoons olive oil
- 3 eggs
- 200g (7oz) ground almonds
- 50g (2oz) chopped nuts (you could use walnuts, hazelnuts, Brazil nuts or almonds, or a mixture)

You'll also need

- 20cm (8in) round tin
- greaseproof paper

ICA Tip

You could make the cake in advance in and cut it into quarters before freezing, so that you have handy portions to defrost as needed.

1. Preheat oven to 150°C/300°F/Gas 2. Line a 20cm (8in) round tin with greaseproof paper.

2. Combine all the ingredients except the ground and chopped nuts, and stir well. Then stir in the ground and chopped nuts. Spoon evenly into the lined tin.

3. Bake in the preheated oven for 90 minutes. Check to see whether the cake is done by inserting a skewer into the centre: the cake is done if the skewer comes out clean. If the cake is still wet, bake for up to a further 30 minutes.

4. Remove from the oven and allow to cool before removing from the tin.

Goan Christmas Cake

ALOMA MCKAY, ENNISTYMON GUILD, CLARE

This is my mother's recipe for Christmas cake. I grew up in Bangladesh but originally come from Goa, a former Portuguese colony on the west coast of India. We always made this cake at Christmastime, mixing it in a huge steel bowl, about 1½ foot wide, with a gigantic 2-foot long wooden spoon. I've reduced the quantities here.

Makes a 25cm (10in) cake

- 450g (1lb) butter
- 450g (1lb) sugar
- 12 large eggs (preferably free range), separated
- 225g (8oz) plain white flour
- 3 teaspoons baking powder
- 1 whole nutmeg, grated (or 3 teaspoons ground nutmeg)
- 225g (8oz) semolina
- 2 teaspoons vanilla extract
- 350g (12oz) sultanas
- 350g (12oz) currants
- 350g (12oz) raisins
- 175g (6oz) mixed peel
- 225g (8oz) almonds, chopped
- 2 tablespoons caraway seeds

To finish

- See pages 124–127 for icing and marzipan recipes and ideas

You'll also need

- 25cm (10in) cake tin
- baking parchment
- brown paper

1. Preheat oven to 140°C/275°F/Gas 1. Grease and line the cake tin with a double thickness of baking parchment.

2. In a large mixing bowl, beat the butter and sugar until light and fluffy. Add the egg yolks and beat well. Sieve in the flour, baking powder and nutmeg, folding in as you go, and then fold in the semolina. Mix well.

3. In a separate bowl, beat the egg whites well, then add to the flour mixture. Stir in the vanilla extract, then add the dried fruit, mixed peel, almonds and caraway seeds. Stir gently until all the ingredients are well mixed.

4. Spoon into the greased and lined tin. Tie a double band of brown paper around the outside of the tin to prevent the cake drying out in the oven.

5. Bake in the preheated oven for about 3–3½ hours. To check if it is cooked, insert a skewer into the centre of the cake: the cake is done if the skewer comes out clean.

6. Remove from the oven and allow to cool before removing from the tin. Wrap in baking parchment and transfer to an airtight container. Store in a cool, dark place. The cake will keep for up to a month.

ICA *Tip*

An airtight cake tin is better for long-term storage than a plastic container, as there is less chance of contamination of flavour.

MISS FOGARTY'S CHRISTMAS CAKE

'Miss Fogarty's Christmas Cake' is a song written by the American Charles Frank Horn in 1883. Over the years it has done the rounds in various formats. One of these versions, 'Miss Hoolihan's Christmas Cake', was sold as a penny broadsheet on the streets of Victorian Dublin. A very young James Joyce sang a version of it at a fundraiser at Bray Boat Club. He was just six years old, and had yet to be persuaded that a singing career was not for him. (It is said that being beaten by tenor John McCormack at the Feis Ceoil made that decision for him.)

As I sat in my window last evening,
The letterman brought it to me
A little gilt-edged invitation sayin'
'Gilhooley come over to tea'
I knew that the Fogarties sent it.
So I went just for old friendship's sake.
The first thing they gave me to tackle
Was a slice of Miss Fogarty's cake.

Chorus:
There was plums and prunes and cherries
There was citrons and raisins and cinnamon too
There was nutmeg, cloves and berries
And a crust that was nailed on with glue
There were caraway seeds in abundance
Such that work up a fine stomach ache
That could kill a man twice after eating a slice
Of Miss Fogarty's Christmas cake

Miss Mulligan wanted to try it,
But really it wasn't no use
For we worked at it over an hour
And we couldn't get none of it loose
Till Murphy came in with a hatchet
And Kelly came in with a saw
That cake was enough be the powers above
For to paralyse any man's jaw.

[Chorus]

Miss Fogarty sat proud as a peacock
Kept smiling and blinking away
Till she tripped over Flanagans brogans
And she spilt a whole brewin' of tay
Aye Gilhooley she says you're not eatin,
Try a little bit more for me sake
And no Miss Fogarty says I,
For I've had quite enough of your cake.

[Chorus]

Maloney was took with the colic,
O'Donald's a pain in his head
McNaughton lay down on the sofa,
And he swore that he wished he was dead,
Miss Bailey went into hysterics
And there she did wriggle and shake,
And everyone swore they were poisoned
Just from eating Miss Fogarty's cake.

[Chorus]

– C. Frank Horn

Light Plum Pudding

BREEGE QUINN, ENNYBEGS GUILD, LONGFORD

This light pudding is based on a recipe I originally found in the November 1974 edition of the Irish Farmers' Journal, *and which I have perfected over the years. It's been so popular with my family that I now make a pudding for each of my children every Christmas.*

Makes 1 large or 2 small puddings

- 225g (8oz) butter
- 225g (8oz) brown sugar
- 50g (2oz) plain flour
- 225g (8oz) breadcrumbs
- 3 eggs, beaten
- ½ teaspoon baking powder
- 110g (4oz) currants
- 110g (4oz) sultanas
- 110g (4oz) raisins
- 110g (4oz) chopped apple
- 50g (2oz) mixed peel
- 50g (2oz) glacé cherries
- ½ teaspoon nutmeg
- ¼ teaspoon mixed spice
- ½ orange, grated zest and juice
- about 75ml (6fl.oz) stout
- 125ml (4fl oz) whiskey (or white rum, which is also delicious)

You'll also need

- 1 large or 2 small pudding bowls
- greaseproof paper or baking parchment
- tinfoil
- twine

1. In a large mixing bowl, beat the butter and sugar to a smooth cream with a wooden spoon.

2. Fold in the flour and breadcrumbs, alternating with the beaten eggs until well incorporated. Add the baking powder, dried fruit, apple, mixed peel, glacé cherries, spices and orange zest and mix well. Stir in the orange juice, stout and whiskey.

3. Transfer the mixture to a pudding bowl and cover the top of the mixture with 2 pieces of greaseproof paper or baking parchment. Then cover the bowl with tinfoil, so that the foil comes about 5cm (2in) above the sides of the bowl, and tie with twine.

4. Place in a saucepan of simmering water. Cover the saucepan and leave the pudding to steam for 4–5 hours (or about 2–2½ hours if using a pressure cooker). The water should come no more than halfway up the bowl, and may need to be topped up periodically.

5. If you're in a hurry, you can divide the mixture between 2 small pudding bowls and steam each pudding in separate saucepans, thereby halving the cooking time for each.

ICA Tip

If you have the time, it's worth combining the dried fruits and orange zest in a delph bowl with the whiskey or rum, covering and soaking overnight before mixing the pudding.

Rich Plum Pudding

MARY O'GORMAN, MAYNOOTH GUILD, KILDARE

I have been making this suet-based pudding since I married over 30 years ago. It is my mother-in-law's recipe. I still make one every year for my sisters and sisters-in-law. The addition of carrot darkens and sweetens the pudding.

Makes 2 large puddings

- 285g (10oz) breadcrumbs
- 225g (8oz) shredded suet
- 110g (4oz) flour
- 1 dessertspoon mixed spice
- ½ teaspoon grated nutmeg
- 225g (8oz) brown sugar
- 50g (2oz) ground almonds
- 1 large cooking apple
- 1 carrot
- 110g (4oz) whole almonds, blanched and roughly chopped
- 350g (12oz) sultanas
- 225g (8oz) raisins
- 175g (6oz) currants
- 110g (4oz) mixed peel
- 110g (4oz) glacé cherries, halved
- 1 small orange, grated zest and juice
- 1 lemon, grated zest and juice
- 4 eggs
- 1 tablespoon treacle
- 1 small teaspoon bicarbonate of soda
- 1 tablespoon vinegar
- 1 standard wineglass of any spirit you like
- 330ml (11fl.oz.) stout or ale (or milk if you prefer)

You'll also need

- 2 large pudding bowls
- greaseproof paper
- tinfoil
- twine

1. In a large mixing bowl, combine the breadcrumbs and shredded suet. Sieve in the flour together with the spices and stir in the sugar and ground almonds.

2. Peel and grate the apple and carrot and add to the mixture, along with the chopped almonds, sultanas, raisins, currants, mixed peel, halved glacé cherries and grated zest of the orange and lemon. Add the juice of the orange and lemon and mix well.

3. Beat the eggs and melt the treacle, and stir them both into the bowl. Dissolve the bicarbonate of soda in the vinegar and add to the mixture together with your spirit of choice. Stir well. Add a little stout, ale or milk to moisten the mixture, just enough to make a consistency that drops heavily from the spoon. Mix thoroughly.

4. Cut 2 circles of greaseproof paper to place in the base of each pudding bowl. Divide the mixture equally between the 2 bowls. Cover each bowl with 2 circles of greaseproof paper and then one piece of tinfoil, and tie with twine to secure.

5. Place each pudding in a separate saucepan of simmering water, cover and simmer steadily for 5 hours. A little longer won't hurt, although this makes for a much darker pudding. Make sure that the water comes no more than halfway up the bowl and top up periodically to ensure that the water does not boil off.

6. After steaming, remove the top covers and transfer to a warm oven for 10 minutes to dry off. Re-cover each pudding with 2 fresh pieces of greaseproof paper and a fresh piece of tinfoil, and store in a cool dark place. The puddings will keep for at least 12 months.

7. Steam for 2 hours before serving.

Porter Cake

MARY GAVIN, CLIFDEN GUILD, GALWAY

I got this recipe in 1970 from my mother-in-law, Mary, who is now in her 95th year. She loves to have a slice with a small glass of sherry. Over the years, this cake was wrapped in greaseproof paper and sent in suitcases to many different parts of the world. Enjoy!

Makes a 23cm (9in) cake

- 225g (8oz) butter
- 225g (8oz) brown sugar
- 675g (1½lb) mixed dried fruit
- 50g (2oz) dried cherries
- 50g (2oz) mixed peel
- 275ml (½ pint) stout (we always used a bottle of Guinness)
- 450g (1lb) self-raising flour
- 1 teaspoon ground ginger
- 1 teaspoon mixed spice
- ½ teaspoon ground nutmeg
- 3 large eggs, beaten

You'll also need

- 23cm (9in) tin
- baking parchment
- greaseproof paper

1. Preheat oven to 190°C/375°F/Gas 5. Line the cake tin with baking parchment.

2. Combine the butter, sugar, dried fruit, mixed peel and stout in a large saucepan and slowly bring to the boil. Remove from the heat and leave to cool completely.

3. Add the flour, spices and beaten eggs and mix all ingredients together.

4. Transfer to the lined tin and bake in the preheated oven for 1½–2 hours, or until a skewer inserted into the centre of the cake comes out clean.

5. Remove from the oven and allow to cool before removing from the tin. Wrap well in greaseproof paper and store in a cool dark place.

Early Preparations

"*We would look forward for months to the Christmas. During those 1950s summers, we would go searching the woods and by-ways for the 'Christmas Logs'. These were about three foot long and they were used in the open hearth as the special Christmas fire. They were raised up on two big stones so the draught could go under them. When you were sitting there on the most important day of the year, it was pure beautiful. When one log burned down, you put on another.*

The run-up to Christmas was a very exciting time and the arrival of cards in the shop windows was the first sign that Christmas was only around the corner. It was a very busy time in houses all over the country, and one of the first jobs to be done was to have the chimney cleaned – to make access for Santa easier, of course. The next job in our house was cleaning the main room of the house. It had to sparkle.

Decorations were put up and all the pictures on the walls were bedecked with bright green holly. The crib was then given pride of place on the window sill. It was always a great time of the year to catch up on any running repairs that needed to be done around the house."

– Joan Connelly, Templemore Guild, Tipperary

Start by doing what's necessary;
then do what's possible;
and suddenly you are doing the impossible.

– Saint Francis of Assisi

Making a List

Once you have the pudding prepared and the cakes baked, it's time to think about making lists, so that when the time comes to check them twice, you know you've got everything covered.

Consider keeping a special Christmas notebook that you can take out every year in mid-November, to remind you of all the details you might otherwise have forgotten from previous years. Take note of what you need to buy and, more important, what not to buy – there can be so much food wastage at this time of year.

Include in your 'little book of Christmas' your Christmas card list and addresses. You might also start a list of presents given to friends and family in recent years, to avoid the disappointment of giving similar presents year after year to the same person. (We all know that it happens!)

Then it's time to make a list of what needs doing to get the house ready for Christmas – a big job if left until the last weeks in December, but less so if you get organised early. It's even easier if you delegate, and get all the family involved in preparation and cleaning for the special season.

Traditionally every room in the house would get a good cleaning and even a touch of paint where needed. Linens, furniture, pots and pans would be washed and scoured or polished until they were sparkling. Even the outhouses might get a splash of whitewash (a mixture of water and lime).

Today we're probably less concerned about our outhouses, but there are still lots of useful jobs you can tick off early, not least of which is stocking the freezer with useful fall-back staples – and maybe some special gluten-free substitutes, just to be extra prepared.

Carrot and Lemon Soup

MAURA RIORDAN, DUN LAOGHAIRE GUILD, DUBLIN

Orange vegetables such as carrots can be a great boost to the immune system during the winter months, so what better kind of soup to have in the freezer? A pretty garnish can transform it into a festive starter.

Serves 8

- 3 tablespoons rapeseed oil
- 900g (2lb) carrots, peeled and chopped
- 1 large onion, peeled and chopped
- 2 large potatoes, peeled and chopped
- 2 garlic cloves, crushed
- 1.75 litres (3 pints) vegetable stock
- 2 vegetable stock cubes
- salt and pepper
- 2 lemons, finely grated zest and juice

To garnish

- roughly chopped herbs (parsley, dill or coriander, or a mixture)
- fresh cream or yoghurt (optional)

1. Heat the oil in a large heavy-based saucepan and add the carrots, onion and potato. Cover the saucepan and gently sweat the vegetables for about 5 minutes, stirring occasionally.

2. Add the garlic, vegetable stock and stock cubes, and season with salt and pepper. Cover again and simmer gently until the vegetables are tender.

3. Allow to cool a little before blending thoroughly.

4. Before serving, stir in the grated lemon zest and then add the juice to taste. Gently reheat and serve sprinkled with a garnish of chopped herbs, and maybe a swirl of cream or yoghurt and a sprinkling of lemon zest for visual effect.

ICA Tip

Freezing in small containers means that you can defrost one or two servings at a time, as needed – perfect for the days after Christmas when family can be coming and going.

Potato and Leek Soup

ANNE MARIA DENNISON, MAINISTIR NA FÉILE GUILD, LIMERICK

This hearty soup is comfort food at its best and it's great on a cold wintery day. We like to make it using lots of potato. It freezes well, making it a great standby. Be sure to cool it fully before freezing and then defrost thoroughly before reheating.

Serves 6

- 1kg potatoes, peeled
- 2–3 large leeks, washed thoroughly
- 1 large onion, peeled
- 50g butter
- 1 litre vegetable stock (cubes will do if you don't have your own)
- salt and pepper

You'll also need

- greaseproof paper

1. Roughly chop the vegetables. Melt the butter in a large heavy-based saucepan over a gentle heat, add the chopped onion and leeks and stir well to coat them in butter.

2. Lay a sheet of greaseproof paper on top of the vegetables and put the saucepan lid on. Sweat the vegetables gently for about 10 minutes, then add the potato and sweat for a further 5 minutes, stirring occasionally.

3. Remove the greaseproof paper and add the stock. Bring to the boil, reduce the heat and simmer, covered, until all vegetables are soft, stirring occasionally.

4. Allow to cool before blending. Season to taste, and thin with more stock if you like a lighter soup. Serve piping hot.

ICA Tip

Keep vegetable trimmings in a freezer bag in the freezer until you have stockpiled enough to use as the base for a vegetable stock. Avoid brassicas like broccoli, and avoid dirty peelings, but trimmings of other vegetables and herb stalks can all go in.

Ribollita Soup

ANNE MARIA DENNISON, MAINISTIR NA FÉILE GUILD, LIMERICK

A very hearty soup that is just the job on a cold winter's day, this can be made well in advance as it freezes well. It's quite versatile, too; it can be left chunky and served with crusty bread for a rustic lunch or supper, or blitzed to a smooth soup and garnished with croûtons for a more elegant starter.

Serves 8–10

- 2–3 tablespoons olive oil
- 2 medium onions, chopped
- 2 large carrots, sliced
- 2 celery sticks, finely sliced
- 1 head of fennel, trimmed and finely sliced (optional)
- 4 cloves garlic, chopped (optional)
- 2 large courgettes, peeled and finely sliced
- 400g tin tomatoes
- 400g tin mixed beans, drained
- 2 tablespoons pesto
- 900ml vegetable or chicken stock
- salt and pepper

To serve

- chopped parsley
- croûtons or crusty bread

1. Heat some olive oil in a large heavy-based saucepan, add the onions, carrots and celery – and the fennel and garlic, if using – and fry gently for 10 minutes.

2. Add the courgettes and cook for 2 minutes before adding the tinned tomatoes, beans, pesto and stock.

3. Bring to the boil, reduce the heat and simmer for 30 minutes or until the vegetables are tender. Add a little more stock if the soup is too thick. You can leave it chunky, or liquidise to make it lovely and smooth.

4. Check seasoning before serving, and garnish with a sprinkling of chopped parsley. Serve with croûtons or crusty bread.

ICA *Tip*

If you are freezing the soup, make sure it is completely cold before you put it in the freezer.

"I was born and raised on a farm in County Offaly in the forties. We lived three and a half miles from the nearest town and our only means of transport was a pony and trap. But we were a mostly self-sufficient family, so it was only necessary for us to go to town every fortnight or so to buy tea, sugar, clothes and, most important, paraffin for the lamp. My father grew all our vegetables and we always had our own meat and poultry: pigs, hens, chickens, geese, turkeys and ducks. Every Christmas we had our own home-reared ham and goose.

We had our own milk, so butter-making was a weekly chore. The milk separator was used every day to separate the cream from the skimmed milk, which was then given to the calves. The cream we put into the end-over-end churn, and we all took our turn at the handle and looking into the glass spy hole on the lid of the churn to check when the butter was made. As there were six of us, we would make bets with one another as to who would have the final turning of the churn. The butter was then taken out, washed in cold water and shaped into pound blocks with butter spades.

The buttermilk was used for making bread and sometimes to drink on its own. My mother made bread every day. Brown bread and soda bread were baked in the 'baker', with coals from the fire put on the lid and underneath the baker. Griddle bread was made with soda bread mixture and baked on a floured hot griddle for about ten minutes on each side.

Bread soda had many other uses in our house – cleaning the cups, knives, forks and spoons; cleaning our teeth; taking stains out of clothes and even furniture.

My mother also made the most delicious homemade jam. I especially loved her rhubarb jam, which she made by steeping equal parts of chopped rhubarb and sugar overnight before adding root ginger and boiling it until it set. We enjoyed the homemade jam all through the winter months.

Growing up in our house, no one complained of boredom! We were never idle, drawing water and turf and all the work that had to be done around the house and on the farm."

– Mary McRedmond, Clara Guild, Offaly

Simple Brown Bread

MARY MCREDMOND, CLARA GUILD, OFFALY

Everybody needs a simple brown bread recipe in their life, and this soda bread is just that. While it takes very little time to prepare, it's handy to have some stored in the freezer for whenever you might need it during the holidays. Slice before freezing for extra convenience.

Serves 6

- 175g (6oz) plain flour
- 1 teaspoon bicarbonate of soda
- ¾ teaspoon salt
- 225g (8oz) wholemeal flour
- 25g (1oz) wheat germ
- 25g (1oz) bran
- about 400ml (¾ pint) buttermilk

1. Preheat oven to 200°C/400°F/Gas 6.
2. Sieve the plain flour, soda and salt into a large mixing bowl. Add the wholemeal flour, wheat germ and bran and mix well.
3. Gradually add enough buttermilk to bring together into a soft dough.
4. Shape into a round, cut a cross in the top and transfer to a floured baking tray.
5. Bake in the preheated oven for 50 minutes or until the base sounds hollow when tapped. Cool on a wire rack.

ICA Tip

If you prefer a softer crust, wrap the bread in a tea towel while it is cooling.

Spelt Bread

ANNE MARIA DENNISON, MAINISTIR NA FÉILE GUILD, LIMERICK

As well as being a healthy alternative to wheat-based bread, spelt bread has great texture and is very filling. It freezes well and so it can be made in advance, sliced before freezing and then defrosted as required. It's the perfect foil for smoked salmon or a good hearty soup.

Makes one 900g (2lb) loaf

- 250g (9oz) wholegrain spelt flour
- 1 teaspoon bicarbonate of soda
- 1 teaspoon cream of tartar, e.g. Bextartar
- ½ teaspoon baking powder
- 200g (7oz) pinhead oatmeal
- 285ml (½ pint) milk (soya milk can be used; it makes no difference to the taste)
- 30ml (2 tablespoons) honey
- 30ml (2 tablespoons) sunflower or rapeseed oil
- 2 eggs, beaten
- 100g (3½oz) chopped walnuts or sesame seeds

You'll also need

- 900g (2lb) loaf tin
- baking parchment

1. Preheat oven to 180°C/350°F/Gas 4. Line a loaf tin with baking parchment.
2. Sieve the flour, bread soda, cream of tartar and baking powder into a large mixing bowl. Add the pinhead oatmeal.
3. Add the wet ingredients, mix well and fold in the walnuts or sesame seeds.
4. Pour into the lined loaf tin and bake in the preheated oven for 45–50 minutes, checking after 40 minutes. If the loaf is browning too fast, cover with greaseproof paper for the last 10 minutes (ovens vary, so this will depend on your oven's temperature).
5. Turn off the oven but leave the bread in the oven to cool slightly before removing it from the tin and wrapping in a tea towel.
6. Allow the bread to cool completely before freezing, either as a whole loaf or sliced.

ICA Tip

Cream of tartar (Bextartar is one brand) is a raising agent that is generally used with bread soda; it's combined with regular milk instead of buttermilk or sour milk.

SALTER

Siobhán's Carrot Cake

ANNE MARIA DENNISON, MAINISTIR NA FÉILE GUILD, LIMERICK

My sister Siobhán's carrot cake is a favourite with family and friends. A moist cake with a lovely texture, the fruit and walnuts make it a delicious alternative to a rich Christmas cake. It also freezes well and can be handy to have as a back-up for the festive season.

Makes one 900g (2lb) loaf or a 23cm (9in) round cake

- 175ml (6fl oz) rapeseed, corn or sunflower oil
- 150g brown sugar or caster sugar
- 1 teaspoon vanilla extract
- 3 medium eggs, beaten
- 150g (5½oz) plain flour
- 1 teaspoon ground cinnamon or ginger
- 1 teaspoon bicarbonate of soda
- 1 teaspoon baking powder
- 1 teaspoon salt
- 200g (7oz) carrot, grated
- 100g (3½oz) walnut pieces
- 125g (4½oz) sultanas or raisins

For the frosting

- 75g (3½oz) soft cream cheese, at room temperature
- 50g (2oz) butter, at room temperature
- ½ teaspoon vanilla extract
- 100g (3½oz) icing sugar, sieved

To decorate

- 1–2 handfuls walnuts, halved or roughly chopped (optional)

You'll also need

- 900g (2lb) loaf tin or 23cm (9in) round cake tin
- baking parchment

1. Preheat oven to 180°C/350°F/Gas 4. Line your tin with baking parchment.

2. In a large mixing bowl, combine the oil, sugar, vanilla extract and eggs and beat well.

3. Gradually sieve in the flour, ground spice, bicarbonate of soda, baking powder and salt, beating well after each addition to ensure that they are well incorporated. Add the grated carrot, walnuts and sultanas or raisins and mix well. Pour the mixture into the prepared tin.

4. Bake in the centre of the preheated oven for about 70 minutes, or until the cake is firm to the touch and a skewer inserted into the centre comes out clean. It may need an extra 5 minutes or so.

5. Remove from the oven and allow to cool in the tin for 5 minutes. Turn out onto a wire rack, remove the paper and leave to cool completely.

6. Meanwhile, combine the cream cheese, butter and vanilla extract in a bowl and mix well. Slowly add the icing sugar and beat until smooth.

7. Once the cake is fully cool, spread the frosting over the top of the cake (and the sides if you wish) and top with walnuts, if using.

ICA Tip

If you prefer, you could place all the ingredients except the walnuts in a food processor and whizz until everything is well mixed, then fold in the chopped walnuts.

White Chocolate and Raspberry Cheesecake

BRIDGID KEANE, ARDMORE GRANGE GUILD, WATERFORD

This cheesecake has become a great favourite in our household at Christmas. It can be made a day or two in advance and freezes well, so I often freeze what is not used to be enjoyed at a later date. But equally you could make it for freezing well ahead of Christmas.

Makes a 20cm (8in) cheesecake

- 175g (6oz) gingernut biscuits, crushed
- 90g (3oz) butter, melted

For the topping

- 400g (14oz) cream cheese
- 60g (2oz) unrefined golden caster sugar
- 1 lemon, finely grated zest only
- 1 tablespoon lemon juice
- 300g (10oz) white chocolate
- 300ml (½ pint) double cream
- 250g (9oz) fresh raspberries

To serve

- 1–2 tablespoons white chocolate curls
- 1–2 handfuls extra raspberries

You'll also need

- 20cm (8in) loose-bottomed round cake tin

1. Mix together the crushed biscuits and melted butter. Press this mixture over the base of a cake tin, and chill in the fridge or freezer.

2. Beat together the cream cheese and sugar with the lemon zest and juice.

3. Melt the white chocolate in a bain marie (a bowl placed over a pan of simmering water). When it has melted, pour it into the cream cheese mixture in a thin stream, whisking as you go.

4. In a separate bowl, whip the cream until it forms soft peaks and fold it, with the raspberries, into the cream cheese mixture.

5. Spoon the mixture over the biscuit base and level the top with a palette knife. Chill the cheesecake for at least 4 hours or overnight. Alternatively, wrap well and freeze until ready to use. Transfer to the fridge and leave overnight to defrost fully before serving.

6. Before serving, decorate with fresh raspberries sprinkled with curls of white chocolate.

ICA *Tip*

A potato peeler is handy for shaving thin curls of white chocolate off a block or bar.

Cranberry and Orange Scone Bread

MAIREAD O'GORMAN, CAMROSS GUILD, WEXFORD

I like to make a loaf with this scone recipe. The contrast between the sweet bread base and the sour berries really makes your tastebuds tingle. It's wonderful for afternoon tea, served with cream laced with a drop of poitín – just enough to give a little twist on the tongue!

Serves 8

- 225g (8oz) cranberries
- 275g (10oz) plain flour
- 100g (3½oz) sugar
- 2 teaspoons baking powder
- ½ teaspoon bicarbonate of soda
- ¼ teaspoon salt
- 1 teaspoon grated orange zest
- 110g (4oz) butter, cubed
- 1 large egg, lightly beaten
- 125ml (4fl oz) buttermilk
- 2 teaspoons orange juice

To finish

- 2 teaspoons milk
- 1 tablespoon sugar

1. Preheat oven to 200°C/400°F/Gas 6. Lightly grease a baking sheet.

2. Toss the cranberries in a tablespoon of flour and set aside.

3. Combine the remaining flour with the sugar, baking powder, soda, salt and orange zest. Cut in the butter, leaving some lumps.

4. Combine the egg, buttermilk and orange juice and add to the flour mixture, stirring with a fork. Stir in the dusted berries.

5. Pat the dough into a circle on the prepared baking sheet. Cut into 8 wedges but do not separate. Brush with milk and sprinkle with sugar. Bake in a preheated oven for 20 minutes until golden brown.

6. Remove from the tray and transfer to a wire rack to cool. If you prefer a soft crust, wrap the bread in a damp cloth while cooling. Wrap well before freezing.

ICA Tip

I love to set a pretty table for afternoon tea, placed by the fireplace or Christmas tree and laid with a patchwork red and white quilt worked in the Irish Chain pattern, with embroidered napkins and tea cosy. Instead of flowers, I prefer to light a candle for extra atmosphere.

Nanny's Christmas Bread

MARY CURLEY, LUCAN GUILD, DUBLIN

My grandmother Sheila O'Connor used to bake this bread in an oven hanging on a crook over an open turf fire with a hot sod of turf on top of the lid. My sons can't get enough of 'Nanny's bread' (see page 187 for photo), and it's now being baked and enjoyed in Vancouver, far from that turf fire in Cahirciveen.

Makes 1 loaf

- 85g (3oz) butter
- 675g (1½ lb) plain white flour
- 1 teaspoon bicarbonate of soda
- 1 teaspoon cream of tartar (e.g. Bextartar)
- 1½ teaspoons mixed spice
- 110g (4oz) Demerara sugar
- 1 fistful currants
- 1 fistful raisins (muscatels, if available)
- 1 fistful sultanas
- 110g (4oz) mixed peel
- 110g (4oz) chopped glacé cherries
- 110g (4oz) flaked almonds
- 3 eggs
- 3 tablespoons treacle
- 500ml (18fl oz) buttermilk, plus a little extra if needed

1. Preheat oven to 200°C/400°F/Gas 6.
2. In a large mixing bowl, rub the butter into the flour to make a crumb-like consistency. Stir in the remaining dry ingredients and the fruit, peel and almonds.
3. Beat the eggs in another bowl, add the treacle and mix well before adding the buttermilk. Add this to the dry ingredients and mix well, adding more buttermilk if needed to bring together into a dough. Turn out onto a floured surface and knead lightly for a few minutes.
4. Shape into a round and place on a floured baking sheet. Bake in a preheated oven for about 45 minutes or until the base sounds hollow when tapped. Turn out onto wire rack to cool fully before slicing.

THE AMERICAN PARCEL

"As children growing up in Cahirciveen in County Kerry, our Christmas excitement would start in the first week of December when my mother would say, 'It's time to write the "Dear John, Christmas is here again" letters.'

She wrote letters and cards to her sister Chrissie in New York, cousins Hannie and Bessie in New Haven, Connecticut and friends in Rhode Island – all very exotic addresses to us. She also wrote to her brother John in London, my Dad's brother Jack, also in London, and several relations and friends all over England. These letters had to be posted early in December. Then she wrote Christmas cards and letters to friends and relations all around Ireland.

We eagerly awaited the arrival of our first Christmas card from America. We loved the sparkly snow scenes as, living beside the sea, we never saw snow like that. We would rush home from school to see what our postman, 'Bobbins', had brought that day. There was such excitement if we smelled camphor as we knew then that he had brought a parcel from our Aunty Chrissie in America. We couldn't wait to get rooting in the box to see what clothes, sweets, toys or books she had sent for my brother, sister and me. There would always be something for our parents, too, maybe a shirt and tie or a pullover for my father and a necklace, dress and nylons for Mom. We would have to air the clothes well to get rid of the 'American smell' of camphor mothballs. We were ready then to show off our Christmas outfits at Christmas Day Mass in Filemore church."

– Mary Curley, Lucan Guild, Dublin

THE TURKEY'S IN THE POST

"I grew up on a farm and have fond memories of Christmas preparations. My mother used to hang the Christmas puddings, wrapped in muslin cloths, from the ceiling in the kitchen from the time they were made until Christmas Day.

But I always knew Christmas was approaching when the poultry was being prepared for the post! Each year my mother sent a turkey to my uncle in London and a chicken to a cousin in Liverpool. The poultry were killed and plucked but not drawn (cleaned out), and then wrapped up with head and feet intact. This task took up the entire kitchen table and both my parents' wrapping skills.

First the bird was wrapped in greaseproof paper, then several pages of the Wicklow People, *then strong brown paper (probably saved over the year from meat purchases), and finally robust string. Plastic bags and Sellotape simply weren't available. The two parcels were then taken into town to the post office.*

In the mid-1950s the cousin from Liverpool wrote thanking my parents for the chicken. She stated that she noticed chickens had become more plentiful to buy in her locality, and although they certainly wouldn't taste anything like the Irish chicken, she felt it wasn't necessary for any more chickens to be posted to her.

The turkey was still despatched to London until, in one New Year's letter, my uncle wrote to say that the turkey had arrived safely but had 'gone off' slightly! This was probably a combination of a mild December and the introduction of heating in the sorting office. All was not lost, however, and they had managed to salvage enough of the bird which, having been roasted extra well, provided a hearty dinner without any ill effects.

Needless to say, this all happened long before refrigeration, EU regulations and best before dates."

– Heather Evans, Clonakenny Guild, Tipperary

Sending Christmas Cards

For many years sending and receiving Christmas cards and gifts was a crucial part of an Irish Christmas, especially as so many of what we now call the diaspora lived in far-flung parts of the world. All sorts of things were sent and received in the post, but even the act of sending the annual Christmas card was – and remains – a precious ritual for many.

> *"In my childhood my siblings and I were helped to make our own Christmas cards, gifts and decorations in the kitchen for weeks before the festive season. We generally made them from whatever recycled materials that seemed to 'have potential' (in my mind's eye). I still remember the excitement when a project was finished. Advent was a very happy time for us."*
>
> – *Connie McEvoy, Termonfeckin Guild, Louth*

The custom of sending Christmas cards feels as though it has been around for ever, but it originated in the mid-nineteenth century, when the first card was designed by Sir Henry Cole and his artist friend John Horsley. As printing methods improved, larger quantities were produced and the idea caught on. The earliest Christmas cards usually featured a nativity scene, and it was not long before robin redbreasts and snowy scenes were introduced.

There is still something special about receiving a homemade card. If you want to make up a batch of cards, there are some very simple ideas that you could easily do with some card stock picked up from a craft shop, and a little glue and glitter. You could experiment with shop-bought stamps or stencils (see page 35 for a slightly more ambitious project) or simply make your own seasonal stamp with a good old-fashioned potato stencil. One of the advantages of making your own cards is that you get to choose your own personal seasonal greeting too.

The only cards that really count
Are that extremely small amount
From real friends who keep in touch
And are not rich but love us much.

– John Betjeman, from 'Advent 1955'

Cross-Stitch Christmas Card

CAROLINE POWER, RATOATH GUILD, MEATH

My children have grown up with crafts, and no time of the year was busier than Christmas. Every November we would decide whether we would make Christmas cards, wreaths, garlands – or even salt dough decorations for the tree. One year we settled on a cross-stitch Advent calendar. It took us a couple of years to complete, but is still in use today as a lovely wall hanging. This Christmas card is a little less ambitious!

What you'll need

- 14-count Aida fabric, 14.5cm x 10.5cm
- embroidery cotton: red, white, cream, black, dark blue
- cross stitch needle (tapestry needle)
- picture window card and envelope
- glue
- beads (optional)

1. To centre the design on the fabric, fold the fabric in half vertically and horizontally to find the central point. This central point represents the central square on the chart (see pattern) determined by the two small arrows (see top and side of pattern).

2. Begin stitching anywhere, counting from the central square on the chart and the central square marked by the folding of the fabric.

3. Use two strands of cotton for the cross stitch and one strand for the outline back stitch.

4. Finish off the work neatly by weaving in the threads at the back: stray threads (particularly the black) can show through and spoil the finished picture.

5. Beads can be used to embellish parts of Santa, such as his eyes.

6. Secure the finished product into the card window with glue.

ICA *Tip*

Blank cards can be bought from craft shops, good stationery shops and card-making specialists. They can be square or oval, of different sizes, and are sold with envelopes. The height of the Santa is 6.5cm.

Christmas
Christmas Greeting

Stencilled Christmas Card

MARION FERGUSON, CLONES GUILD, MONAGHAN

I've been making greeting cards and wedding invitations for many years. Complex ones can take several hours to produce. This pretty card is more straightforward. It uses two stencils, one for an image and the other for the Christmas greeting. The biggest expense will be the heat gun, which costs about €20 to buy.

What you'll need

- black card stock, for the centrepiece
- white card stock, for the frame
- 20cm x 20cm (8in x 8in) blank greeting card
- metal stencil(s)
- gold stencil paste
- palette knife and spreader plate for paste
- masking tape
- sticky ink pad (e.g. Versamark)
- sponge daubers
- heat gun
- gold leaf (with mottled multi-coloured elements)
- scrubber sponge or old toothbrush
- good-quality double-sided tape
- peel-offs
- glue
- scissors

ICA Tip

You can buy all the materials required over the internet or in a traditional card-making shop. Alternatively, Dublin's annual Knitting and Stitching Show is a great place for picking up materials.

1. Cut an 18cm x 18cm (7in x 7in) square mat of black card stock for the centrepiece of your Christmas card. Cut a slightly larger square (19cm x 19cm (7.5in x 7.5in)) of white card stock to act as the frame for your centrepiece.
2. Position the first stencil on the black mat and adhere with masking tape. If the tape is very tacky, stick it to your hand or clothes first to remove some of the tackiness so that it doesn't smudge the card stock when removed.
3. Use a palette knife to apply paste through the stencil to the desired area of the black mat, taking care that it doesn't touch the outer parts of the card stock mat. Spread the paste evenly with the spreader plate.
4. Lift off the stencil and, taking care with the sharp points, wash it immediately in warm soapy water and dry. Leave the paste to dry on the black mat before repeating with the second stencil, if using.
5. Once all paste is fully dry, reposition the first stencil directly over the first pasted area and use a sponge dauber to apply Versamark through the stencil onto the dried paste.
6. Remove the stencil and heat the Versamark gently with a heat gun. Quickly scatter gold leaf on the stencilled area, where it will adhere to the heated Versamark. Using a scrubber sponge or old toothbrush, gently brush the gold leaf. It should only adhere to the stencilled area. If using more than one stencil, repeat with the gold leaf for the second pasted area.
7. Stick double-sided tape to all 4 edges of the white mat of card stock, and apply gold leaf to the tape.
8. To assemble the card, place double-sided sticky tape or glue on the back of the black mat and position it in the centre of the white mat so that it is now framed by the gold leaf. Embellish as desired with peel-offs.
9. Finally, mount your framed centrepiece on the blank card with glue or sticky tape.

Advent Calendar

ANNE PAYNE, PORTLAOISE GUILD, LAOIS

Who doesn't love an Advent calendar, especially when it's filled with chocolate treats? This simple little DIY felt calendar is a fun way of counting down the days to Christmas, and a nice project to fill a rainy afternoon in late November with the children or grandchildren.

What you'll need

- paper, for making the pattern
- green felt, for the uppermost Christmas tree shape
- red felt, for the background Christmas tree shape and for the numbers
- yellow felt, for the little pockets
- gold felt, for the star
- red embroidery cotton

1. Draw the outline of a Christmas tree on a piece of paper and cut it out to use as a guide for the green felt shapes.

2. Draw a second Christmas tree just a centimetre or two larger than the first, and cut this out to be a guide for the red felt shapes. The red trees will act as a frame for the green trees.

3. Draw the numbers 1–9 to use as guide for cutting out the felt numbers.

4. Cut out the green and red tree shapes, pin the green onto the red and sew into place by tacking with small stitches.

5. Cut out 24 small pockets from the yellow felt, and one star shape from the gold felt.

6. Cut out the required number of figures needed from the red felt: you will need 13 x no.1, 8 x no.2, 3 x no.3, 3 x no.4, 2 x no.5, 3 x no.6, 2 x no.7, 2 x no.8, 2 x no.9.

7. Sew the figures onto the pockets using the red embroidery cotton.

8. Arrange the pockets and star on the tree and sew in place.

9. Fill the pockets with small wrapped chocolates or sweets.

The Pleasure of Giving

If you start planning early enough, you can use lots of simple ideas to make thoughtful homemade gifts. What a treat for your loved one to enjoy that jar of homemade chutney or handmade truffles, to watch those flowers bloom or catch a scent of that pot pourri bag in a drawer, and be reminded in that moment of your love and friendship.

To make homemade pot pourri bags, simply mix your choice of dried flowers (e.g. lavender, heather, marigold, rose buds) with a few drops of pot pourri reviver oil and leave in a covered container for a few days before transferring to a piece of simple muslin or pretty cloth cut with scallop-edged scissors, and tie with a coloured ribbon. Sometimes the simplest of gifts can become the most treasured items, for example a pretty hardback notebook for recording important life events.

"When I was married in 1991, I was given a Christmas book. At the back of the book, after each Christmas, I wrote a short paragraph about the year that had just passed. I recorded our family highs and lows: births and deaths, pregnancies and first steps. 'We bought a house.' Happy and sad memories were captured in a few words every year. Now we spend a quiet few minutes at Christmas re-reading these words and reflecting upon the time that has passed."

– Stephanie Igoe, Ennybegs Guild, Longford

If you are green-fingered, consider planting up some hyacinth bulbs, which can be forced to flower in winter. Ask at your local garden centre for special heat-treated bulbs – they should have a choice of colours and will give you advice on planting and looking after them. They should be started indoors in a cool dark place such as a garage and later moved to an indoor windowsill. They usually flower about ten weeks after planting, which means that you'll need to be very organised to get them flowering in time for Christmas; but even if you didn't plant them until November, they would brighten a loved one's February.

Or if you want to plan ahead for next Christmas, you could propagate some Christmas cacti in springtime to be in full bloom by next winter.

And of course, with knitting back in vogue, it's a great time to reclaim old traditions of knitting socks or leg cosies (see page 42) for loved ones, or even a fun tea cosy for that extra bit of festive cheer (see page 40).

Be sure to do justice to your time and effort and wrap up your homemade gifts as prettily as possible. The cost of ribbons and wrapping paper can add up, so keep a box for recycling anything that comes your way. Even an old shoebox covered with coloured paper, stuffed with tissue and tied with a bow can look very impressive!

"My Grandma Kavanagh would knit fawn knee socks with beautiful brown crochet turn-down top edgings for all of her grandchildren at Christmas. The girls adored them but the boys weren't as impressed and only wore them (under duress) when she came to visit, happy to let the girls claim them afterwards!

I was an avid learner as a child and enjoyed all crafts. In the days (pre-tissues) when hankies were regarded as a most useful and acceptable Christmas gift, Mam and I made all sorts of pretty sachets to keep them tidy in and included them as part of the gift. One year we knitted berets or jelly bags for everyone. Another year, when needles were scarce, I knitted stockings on bicycle spokes!"

– Connie McEvoy, Termonfeckin Guild, Louth

Christmas Pudding Tea Cosy

MAI KELLY, MOYDOW GUILD, LONGFORD

My sister in London sent me this crocheted tea cosy as a gift. She picked up the pattern in a magazine in London but it was mislaid years ago, so I counted the stitches from the tea cosy for the pattern below. It looks very pretty on the table at Christmas time.

What you'll need

- 6mm crochet hook
- 4mm crochet hook
- ½ ball double knitting black yarn
- ½ ball double knitting brown yarn
- a little coloured yarn: white, red and green
- stuffing
- sewing needles and thread

Abbreviations

- ch = chain
- dc = double crochet
- dk = double knit
- st = stitch
- ss = slip stitch
- tr = treble

For the brown pudding pieces (make two the same)

1. Using a 6mm crochet hook and one strand each of black and brown, dk together. Ch 28.
2. Row 1: 1dc in each d across row (28).
3. Row 2: 1ch, 1dc in each dc across row (28).
4. Row 3: 3ch, 2tr in first dc, miss 2dc, 1dc in next dc (miss 2dc, 5tr into next dc, miss 2dc, 1dc in next dc) 4 times.
5. Row 4: 3ch, 2tr into first dc (miss 2tr, ldc in next tr, miss 2tr, 5tr in next dc) 4 times, 1 dc in 3ch.
   Repeat row 4 seven more times.
6. Break off yarn.
7. Make second side of pudding.

For the white icing

1. Using 6mm crochet hook and 2 swends of where dk together, join yarn to right side of one pudding piece.
2. Row 1: 1ch * miss 2tr, 5tr in dc, miss 2tr, 1dc in next tr * repeat from * to * 3 times, miss 2tr, into last dc of first pudding piece and first dc of second pudding piece at same time, work 5tr (will join pieces), miss 2tr, 1dc in next tr, repeat from * to * 4 times, but on last dc pick up last dc on each pudding piece to join.
3. Row 2: 3ch, 4tr in same space (miss 2tr, 1dc in next tr, miss 2tr, 5tr in next dc) eight times, miss 2tr, ldc in next tr, SL57 to join with 3ch.

4. Row 3: 3ch, 1tr in same space (miss 2tr 1dc in next tr, miss 2tr, 2tr in next dc) 8 times, miss 2tr, ldc in next tr, ss to 3ch to join (27sts).

5. Row 4: 1ch, 1dc in same sp (2dc 10g, 3dc) repeat to last st, 1dc, ss to join (22s)

6. Row 5: 1ch, 1dc in same sp (2dc 10g, 2dc) repeat to last st, 1dc, ss to join (17s)

7. Row 6: 1ch, ldc in same sp (2dc 10g, 1dc) repeat to last st 1dc, ss to join (12s)

8. Row 7: 1ch, (2dc 10g) to end 6st.

9. Break yarn leaving a long tail, catch all 6st remaining and pull tightly to close top. Sew the dc on the brown pudding at base together at sides.

10. Sew in all ends.

For the green holly leaves (make 3)

1. Using 4mm crochet hook and green dk. Ch10.

2. Row 1: 1dc in second ch from hook,* 1htr, 1tr, 3ch, ss to 3rd ch from hook, 3tr, 3ch, ss to 3rd ch from hook, 1tr, 1htr, ldc *, 3ch, ss no 3rd ch from hook, turn and work back along ch, 1dc in first dc, repeat from * to *.

3. Break yarn.

4. Repeat twice.

For the red berries (makes 3):

1. Make a magic circle using 4mm crochet hook and red dk.

2. Row 1: 6dc into circle and pull right, ss to join*

3. Row 2: 1ch, 2dc into each dc, ss to join (12)

4. Row 3: 1ch, 1dc in each dc, ss to join

5. Row 4: 1ch, 1dc in each dc, ss to join

6. Row 5: 1ch (2dc 10g) 10 and ss to join (6)

7. Break yarn, leaving a long tail for sewing.

8. Repeat twice.

9. Stuff berries lightly and sew ends together.

10. Sew leaves and berries to top of tea cosy.

Lollers (Foot–Leg Cosies)

CONNIE MCEVOY, TERMONFECKIN GUILD, LOUTH

From the age of about three or four in the mid-1940s, I was fascinated by the colours, textures and designs of these pretty and practical 'must-haves'. These days, my granddaughters love them as Christmas 'surprise gifts' (see photo on page 118).

What you'll need

- 2 x 25g balls 4-ply burgundy wool
- 1 x 25g ball 4-ply green wool
- pair of no. 11 needles
- pair of no. 6 needles
- tapestry needle for stitching

Abbreviations

- k = knit
- p = purl
- st = stitch
- tog. = together
- st. st. = stocking stitch (1 row knit, 1 row purl)
- sl = slip

Tension

- 6 stitches x 7 rows = 2.5cm (1in) measured over stocking stitch using no. 6 needles.

1. Both foot–leg cosies are worked in the same way.
2. Using the burgundy yarn and no. 11 needles, cast on 64 sts. Work 6 rows in k1 p1 rib.
3. Change to no. 6 needles and continue as follows: *
4. 1st row: k twice into every st (128 sts).
5. 2nd row: sl 1 then p to last st. K1.
6. Work 4 rows in st. st.
7. 7th row: k2 tog. to end of row (64 sts).
8. Join in the green yarn and work 5 rows in k1 p1 rib.*
9. Rejoin the burgundy yarn, repeat from * to *, then from * to 7th row, once (64 sts).
10. Change to no. 11 needles and work 6 rows in k1 p1 rib. Cast off loosely.

To assemble

11. Join the cast-off and cast-on edges together at wrong side of work. Try to have one half of the cast-off edge stitches visible at the right side of the work as they will come in useful when weaving in the green yarn (loops for decorative purposes down the front of cosies if desired). If this venture is not successful, simply work a row of running stitches down the front seam instead.
12. You will now have a tube and all that remains to be done is to stitch up one end for the toes.
13. The increase and decrease pattern plus rib sections automatically provides a pretty scallop top edge. Because I had ample green yarn at the finish, I worked a row of buttonhole stitches which can help to emphasise this (but is optional).

LOLLERS BY LAMPLIGHT

"These 'lollers' were mostly produced at night-time by the light of an oil lamp. In our farmhouse my late father would look up the chimney at about 9 p.m. each night to predict if we were going to get frost before morning, depending on what stars were visible from his fireside chair. My mother would play Irish dance music on the melodeon so we could warm ourselves up before going to bed, and my siblings and I looked forward to the fun of knocking icicles from the barn roof in the morning.

In the days before central heating, 'lollers' were invaluable from late autumn to late spring. Open fires had a tendency to roast the fronts of those gathered in search of warmth while their backs were often very cold. These knitted cosies protected the lower leg and ankle from chilblains and draughts from behind, while protecting the shins from the heat of the roaring fire. They also served as bed socks, plus protection if hot water bottles were too hot to begin with. Some ladies even had matching tea cosies for when breakfast was served to them in bed!"

– Connie McEvoy, Termonfeckin Guild, Louth

Knitted Santa Claus

HELEN KAVANAGH, BORRIS-IN-OSSORY GUILD, LAOIS

This little knitted Santa Claus stands 23cm (9in) tall when complete. He makes an ideal stocking filler or little gift for a young child. I knit them for the shoe boxes that we fill with goodies for needy children abroad each Christmas.

What you'll need

- 4mm (8) needles
- 50g ball red double knitting wool
- small amount each of white, black and pink double knitting wool
- flame-resistant polyester stuffing

Abbreviations

- k = knit
- p = purl
- ss = slip stitch
- st = stitch
- st. st. = stocking stitch (1 row knit, 1 row purl)
- tog. = together

1. Cast on 8 sts in black and work 10 rows. Change to red and k 14 rows. Break off wool and cast on 8 sts in black. Repeat to form other leg. K across both legs (16 sts) and complete 14 rows.

2. Cast on 12 sts at the beginning of the next 2 rows to form the arms. Work 8 rows. Cast off 12 sts at the beginning of the next 2 rows. Now work 38 rows in body colour (pink) on these 16 sts.

3. Change back to red and cast on 12 stitches at the beginning of the next 2 rows. Work 8 rows. Cast off 12 stitches at the beginning of the next 2 rows. Work 14 rows.

4. Using only the first 8 sts, work 14 rows, change to black and work 10 rows, then cast off. Return to the remaining 8 sts and work 14 rows in red and 10 rows in black, then cast off.

5. To sew up and fill, begin by folding the knitted piece in half lengthways. The fold becomes the top of the head. Join seam around body, leaving a small gap between the legs to insert the stuffing. Turn right-side out. Stuff and then stitch up the gap. Embroider mouth and eyes using black wool.

6. Take a double thickness of pink wool and thread round the neck, going in every few stitches (make sure no loops are left hanging loose). Draw wool tight to form neck and secure ends.

For the beard

1. Cast on 2 sts. Work in garter st and increase 1 stitch at each end of every row until there are 20 sts. Garter st 6 rows.
2. K1 k2 tog. to last st. K1 – 11 sts.
3. K1 row.
4. K1 k2 tog. to end – 6 sts.
5. K1 row.
6. Cast off.

For the hat

1. Using white wool, cast on 36 stitches and garter st 6 rows. Change to red and work 6 rows in stocking stitch.
2. K2 k2 tog. to end (27 stitches). SS 3 rows.
3. K2 k2 tog. to end (21 stitches). SS 3 rows.
4. K2 k2 tog. to end (16 stitches). SS 3 rows. K7 K2tog K7. Purl next and every alternative row.
5. Next row: k6 k2 tog. K7.
6. Next row: k6 k2 tog. K6.
7. Next row: k6 k2 tog. K5.
8. Next row: k5 k2 tog. K5. K2 tog. K5.
9. Next row: k5 k2 tog. K5. K2 tog. K4.
10. Next row: k4 k2 tog. K4.
11. Next row: k4 k2 tog. K3.
12. Next row: k3 k2tog. K3.
13. Next row: k3 k2 tog. K2.
14. Next row: k2 k2 tog. K2.
15. Next row: k2 k2 tog. K1.
16. Next row: k1 k2 tog. K1.
17. Next row: k2 tog. K1.
18. Next row: k2 tog. and fasten off.

For the pom-pom

1. Using white, cast on 12 sts and p 1 row. Then k 1 row. Cast off and roll up tightly to form a little ball.
2. Sew around the edges to secure and attach to the pointed end of hat. Stitch the hat to Santa's head, fold down the pointed end and stitch to side of head. Sew beard to bottom of face and use black to embroider the eyes and mouth.

For the belt

1. Cast on 46 sts in black. Cast off. Sew around Santa's body and embroider a buckle using yellow wool.

Grandma's Filled Christmas Cookies

JOANN LENEHAN, ANNASCAUL GUILD, KERRY

My grandmother showed me how to make this recipe when I was 16. She was born in 1882 and passed away in 1974. I have continued to bake this recipe each Christmas in her memory – and also because my family love it and so do I! I keep the recipe (written in her hand) in my recipe box and enjoy taking it out every Christmas.

Makes 18–20 cookies

- 450g (1lb) butter
- 450g (1lb) caster sugar
- 4 eggs, added one at a time
- 150ml (¼ pint) condensed milk
- 375g (13oz) plain flour
- 1 teaspoon baking powder
- 1 teaspoon vanilla extract

To finish

- 170g (6oz) sultanas, chopped
- 125g (4½oz) chopped nuts
- 200g glacé cherries, cut in half
- jar of redcurrant jelly
- 1 heaped teaspoon ground cinnamon
- 75g (2½oz) caster sugar

You'll also need

- 15cm x 10cm (6in x 4in) baking tray with raised lip

1. To make the dough, mix the ingredients in a large mixing bowl and bring together into a rich dough. Divide in half and refrigerate overnight.
2. In the morning, grease the baking tray and flour lightly. Preheat oven to 170°C/325°F/Gas 3.
3. On a floured surface, roll out one half of the dough so that it is large enough to cover the baking tray. Lay it in the prepared tray. Sprinkle over all the sultanas, but just half each of the nuts and cherries. Drop about 15 teaspoons of redcurrant jelly on the layer.
4. Roll out the second piece of dough and place on top of the first layer. Top with the remaining nuts and cherries. Sprinkle with cinnamon and sugar.
5. Bake in the preheated oven for 40–45 minutes, or until a skewer inserted in the centre comes out clean.
6. Allow to cool before cutting on the diagonal to make diamond shapes.

Rocky Road Fudge

STEPHANIE IGOE, ENNYBEGS GUILD, LONGFORD

We always had fudge at Christmas when I was a child. This recipe is very easy and kids love it. Don't be tempted to substitute evaporated milk for condensed milk.

Makes about 16 pieces

- 350g (12oz) dark chocolate
- 2 tablespoons butter
- 1 x 397g can sweetened condensed milk
- 250g (9oz) mini marshmallows, preferably white only
- 2–3 generous handfuls unsalted peanuts or walnuts, roughly chopped (you could also use dry roasted peanuts)

You'll also need

- 23cm x 32.5cm (9 x 13in) baking tray with raised lip
- baking parchment

1. Line the baking tray with baking parchment.

2. In a heavy saucepan, melt the chocolate over a low heat with the butter and condensed milk. Remove from the heat and allow to cool a little.

3. In large mixing bowl, combine the nuts and marshmallows. Fold in the chocolate mixture.

4. Spread into the lined pan and chill for 2 hours or until firm.

5. Remove from the pan, peel off the paper and cut into squares.

ICA Tip

Store at room temperature, covered, if serving within a day or two. Alternatively, store in an airtight container – the fudge will keep at room temperature for a week or two– or in a fridge for up to three weeks.

Speculoos Biscuit Tree Decorations

MIRIAM MURPHY, BLANCHARDSTOWN GUILD, DUBLIN

These Dutch spiced shortbread biscuits are traditionally served on St Nicholas's feast day on 6 December. They also make lovely tree decorations, if they last that long. Children love making (and eating!) them and the baking aromas evoke everything that is warm and festive about Christmas.

Makes 10–15 biscuits

- 200g (7oz) plain flour
- 2 teaspoons ground cinnamon
- 1 teaspoon ground nutmeg
- 1 teaspoon ground cloves
- 1 teaspoon baking powder
- ½ teaspoon salt
- 100g (3½oz) soft brown sugar
- 1 tablespoon milk
- 150g (5½oz) butter, at room temperature

To finish

- 10–15 pieces of ribbon, about 35cm (14in) long

You'll also need

- baking tray
- baking parchment

1. Preheat oven to 180°C/350°F/Gas 4. Line the baking tray with baking parchment.

2. Sieve the flour, spices, baking powder and salt into a bowl. Add the brown sugar, breaking up any lumps with your hands. Add the milk and butter to bring the mixture together into a dough. Transfer to the fridge to rest for 30 minutes.

3. Turn out the dough onto a lightly floured work surface and roll to about 5mm thickness. Cut out the biscuits with a cookie cutter of your choice, or into whatever shape you like. If you wish to hang them on the tree, use a piping tip nozzle with a 3–4mm opening to cut out a hole at one end of each biscuit. These holes will be used to thread the ribbon through when the biscuits have been baked and cooled.

4. Place the biscuits on the lined baking tray with a gap of at least 2–3cm (1in) between them. Bake in the preheated oven for 15–18 minutes or until golden brown and firm to the touch. Transfer to a wire rack to cool.

5. Thread the ribbons, if using, through the holes in the biscuits and tie the ends together before hanging on your Christmas tree.

6. These biscuits will keep well for up to a week in an airtight container.

ICA Tip

In the Netherlands, a textured or patterned rolling pin is traditionally used to imprint patterns on the dough when it is rolled out.

christmas
of a white

Pistachio and Cranberry Chocolates

PATRICIA CARBIN, BALLINODE GUILD, MONAGHAN

This is a simple enough idea but it looks great. It's versatile, too; you can use whatever dried fruit and nuts you fancy, or candied peel is also good. These chocolates make gorgeous little gifts and are a perfect pick-me-up with a mid-afternoon coffee.

Makes about 40

- 200g (7oz) white chocolate
- 75g (3½oz) shelled pistachios (or whatever nuts you like)
- 50g (2oz) dried cranberries (or whatever dried fruit you like, or a mixture of dried fruit and candied peel)
- 50g (2oz) dark chocolate

You'll also need

- shallow baking tray
- baking parchment

1. Line the base and sides of the baking tray with baking parchment.

2. Break the white chocolate into pieces into a bain marie (a heatproof bowl set over a gently simmering saucepan of water) and gently melt, stirring regularly. Stir in the nuts and fruit, and pour into the prepared tin.

3. Allow to cool while you melt the dark chocolate in a bain marie. Once the white chocolate has cooled but not fully set, pour over the melted dark chocolate. Set aside to cool fully.

4. Cut into small shapes of your choice (e.g. squares or triangles; or diamonds can look pretty).

5. These chocolates will keep well in a cool, dark place or in the fridge. Store them in an airtight container layered with greaseproof paper until you are ready to gift-wrap them. Little packages of clear cellophane tied with a bow look pretty.

Irish Cream Truffles

MARY SHERRY, BALLINODE GUILD, MONAGHAN

These little truffles are delicious served with after dinner coffee on Christmas day, or they make a lovely homemade gift.

Makes approximately 24–30

- 110g (4oz) chocolate, dark or milk
- 2 dessertspoons strong black coffee, hot
- 50g (2oz) butter, flaked
- 1 dessertspoon Irish cream liqueur
- 1 dessertspoon double cream
- 50g (2oz) ground almonds

To finish

- unsweetened cocoa powder, sieved

1. Break up the chocolate into pieces and, in a small pan, melt it to a thick cream with the hot coffee.

2. Remove the pan from the heat and blend in the butter, spoonful by spoonful. Stir in the Irish cream liqueur, double cream and ground almonds. Mix thoroughly, allow to cool and chill until firm.

3. Roll teaspoonfuls of the mixture into small balls and toss in the cocoa to coat them, coating twice if necessary.

4. Shake off any excess cocoa and place in small paper cases.

ICA Tip

If stored in the fridge, these fresh truffles have a relatively short shelf life of about three days from being made, but that can be extended by freezing them on the day you make them. They will take about four hours to defrost.

MINCEMEAT IN PENNIES

"I came across this handwritten recipe in my mother Betty's cookery book, dated 1966. I believe it was a family recipe that she got from her father. Interestingly, in the years 1971 and 1972, when money must have been tight, she priced the ingredients required to make it and compared the cost to shop-bought jars at the time. But of course the homemade version would have tasted so much nicer, as well as being more economical. (I've included in brackets the equivalent prices in euros, to help younger readers translate it into today's context.)"

To make 12lb (roughly 5½kg) mincemeat (euro equivalents in brackets):

Ingredients	**Cost in 1971**	**Cost in 1972**
1lb (450g) suet	20p (25c)	20p (25c)
2lb (900g) brown sugar	12p (15c)	14p (18c)
1lb (450g) currants	22p (28c)	22p (28c)
1lb (450g) raisins	22p (28c)	24p (24c)
4lb cooking apples (1.8kg)	received as a gift	16p (20c)
1oz (25g) grated nutmeg	5p (6c)	6p (8c)
½ grated lemon	(no price given)	

Total cost in 1971:
Cost per pound in the shops was 10p (about 13c today).
Cost per pound homemade was 7p (9c), or 9p (11c) if the apples had to be bought.

Total cost in 1972:
Cost per pound in the shops was 16–18p (20–22c).
Cost per pound homemade was 8½p (11c).

"Mum would have probably used a vegetable suet, like Atora, as my sister is a vegetarian, but shredded animal suet could be used instead. The apples were cored and chopped; no need to peel. She would combine all the ingredients in a large bowl, mix well and cover overnight with a tea towel. The next day she would replace the tea towel with foil and transfer the bowl into a cool oven for a couple of hours, during which time the suet would melt. Then, after a good stir, she would leave the mincemeat to one side to cool fully, stirring occasionally. (Although Mum didn't do it, six tablespoons of brandy could be added to the cold mixture at this stage.) Once it was cold, Mum would fill sterilised jam jars with the mixture and cover with a waxed disc and a lid. It was then ready to store for up to a year in a cool dark place."

– Brenda Leary, Blackrock Guild, Louth

Homemade Mincemeat

ANNE MARIA DENNISON, MAINISTIR NA FÉILE GUILD, LIMERICK

Once you taste homemade mincemeat, you will be slow to use the commercially produced version again. This mincemeat recipe has become a family favourite of ours. It is 'cooked' in a cool oven to prevent fermentation, so it can be made well in advance of Christmas. It makes an ideal Christmas gift.

Makes 2.7kg (6lb), or about 7–8 jars

- 450g (1lb) cooking apples, peeled, cored and grated or chopped
- 450g (1lb) light brown sugar
- 450g (1lb) sultanas
- 450g (1lb) raisins
- 225g (8oz) currants
- 125g (4½oz) glacé cherries, washed and quartered
- 125g (4½oz) ready-to-eat apricots, chopped
- 125g (4½oz) chopped almonds
- 1 orange, grated zest and juice
- 1 lemon, grated zest and juice
- 4 teaspoons mixed spice
- ¼ teaspoon nutmeg
- 250g (9oz) butter, melted
- 6 tablespoons brandy or whiskey

You'll also need

- 8 jam jars
- waxed discs (optional)
- baking parchment
- labels

1. Combine all the ingredients except for the alcohol in a large mixing bowl and mix thoroughly. Cover and allow to stand overnight.

2. The following day, preheat the oven to 110°C/225°F/Gas ¼.

3. Transfer the fruit mixture to a large ovenproof dish or roasting tin.

4. Heat gently in the preheated oven, stirring frequently to prevent sticking. It will take an hour or two, depending on your oven, to heat through thoroughly.

5. Meanwhile, to sterilise your jars, wash well in hot soapy water, rinse thoroughly and place, when still slightly wet, in a microwave on full heat for 60 seconds. Alternatively, boil top-down in a large pot of boiling water for 5 minutes.

6. Remove the mincemeat from the oven and allow it to get completely cold. Stir in the brandy or whiskey and spoon into cool sterilised jars.

7. Seal with waxed discs, cover and label. (If you do not have waxed discs, cut your own from baking parchment.)

8. Label with the date and store in a cool dark place for at least 2 weeks before serving. The mincemeat will keep, and continue improving, for up to 12 months – if it's not all eaten by then!

ICA Tip

If the mincemeat dries out a little after storing for some time, just stir in a little more brandy or whiskey to moisten.

Cranberry Sauce

ANNE MARIA DENNISON, MAINISTIR NA FÉILE GUILD, LIMERICK

This cranberry sauce tastes wonderful and is much fruitier than the shop-bought versions. It is so easy to make and can be made well in advance of Christmas. It also freezes very well, so you could make an extra few batches in late November as gifts for extended family and friends.

Serves 6–8

225g (8oz) brown sugar, or a little more, according to taste
125ml (4fl oz) water
250g (9oz) cranberries, fresh or frozen, washed
2 tablespoons redcurrant jelly
1 orange, zest and juice
125ml (4fl oz) port

1. In a small non-aluminium saucepan, heat the sugar and water until the sugar has dissolved.

2. Add the washed cranberries, bring to the boil and simmer gently for 2 minutes to soften the cranberries. If using frozen cranberries, defrost a little before simmering and only allow a minute or so to soften the berries.

3. Add the redcurrant jelly, orange zest and juice, and simmer for 2 minutes. Remove from the heat, add the port and check for seasoning, adding a little more sugar if desired.

4. This will keep well in the fridge for at least a week, possibly a fortnight, but it also freezes well. Thaw overnight before serving.

Red Onion Jam

MIRIAM MURPHY, BLANCHARDSTOWN GUILD, DUBLIN

This versatile onion jam will keep well for months and makes a great gift. It is especially delicious with patés and terrines, or warmed slightly and served with grilled fish. And there is nothing better with cold turkey and ham on St Stephen's Day.

Makes 450ml (¾ pint)

- 675g (1½lb) red onions
- 110g (4oz) butter
- 150g (5½oz) caster sugar
- 1½ teaspoons coarse sea salt
- ½ teaspoon freshly ground black pepper
- 275ml (½ pint) full-bodied red wine
- 100ml (3½fl oz) sherry vinegar
- 2 tablespoons cassis or port

You'll also need

- jam jars
- waxed discs (optional)
- baking parchment
- labels

1. Peel and thinly slice the onions. Gently heat the butter in a saucepan until it turns a deep brown colour, taking care not to let it burn. Toss in the onions and sugar, season with salt and pepper and stir well.

2. Cover the saucepan and cook for 30 minutes over a gentle heat, keeping an eye on the onions and stirring from time to time with a wooden spoon.

3. Meanwhile, to sterilise your jars, wash well in hot soapy water, rinse thoroughly and place, still slightly wet, in a cool oven for 30 minutes or in a microwave on full heat for 60 seconds. Alternatively, boil top-down in a large pot of boiling water for 5 minutes.

4. Add the remaining ingredients to the onions and cook uncovered for a further 30 minutes over a gentle heat, stirring regularly. For maximum flavour, take care that the mixture doesn't reduce too much too quickly; it should cook very gently.

5. Allow to cool completely, then skim off and discard any fat that has risen to the top.

6. Transfer to cool sterilised jars. Seal with waxed discs, cover and label. (If you do not have waxed discs, cut your own from baking parchment.) Label with the date and store in a cool dark place.

Apricot and Almond Chutney

ANNE HARRINGTON, BLACKROCK GUILD, DUBLIN

My husband's Aunt Nancy first introduced me to the Munster tradition of serving spiced beef at Christmas. This tasty chutney is my addition to the tradition. I picked up the idea from the Bord Bia website. Chutney makes a nice gift too.

Makes 1 litre

- 500ml (18fl oz) wine vinegar
- 450g (1lb) dried apricots, chopped
- 225g (8oz) brown sugar
- 75g (3½oz) almonds, blanched (see page 108) and roughly chopped
- 1 cooking apple, chopped
- 1 onion, chopped
- 2 tablespoons grated fresh root ginger
- ½ tablespoon coriander seeds, toasted and crushed
- dash of Tabasco
- 1–2 teaspoons salt, or to taste

1. Combine all the ingredients in a large non-aluminium saucepan. Heat gently, stirring all the time, until the sugar has dissolved.

2. Simmer for about an hour, but don't overcook. Meanwhile, to sterilise your jars, wash well in hot soapy water, rinse thoroughly and place, still slightly wet, in a microwave on full heat for 60 seconds. Alternatively, boil top-down in a large pot of boiling water for 5 minutes.

3. Remove chutney from the heat, allow to cool slightly and check the seasoning.

4. Spoon into warmed, sterilised jars. Seal immediately with waxed discs, cover and label. (If you do not have waxed discs, cut your own from baking parchment.)

5. Label with the date and store in a cool dark place. The chutney will keep for several months and will improve with time.

ICA Tip

Coriander seeds can be toasted in an oven or in a dry pan – either way, the key is to watch them like a hawk and to use your nose too: you want them somewhere between becoming fragrant and burning.

Chapter 2

Bringing Home Christmas:

A Time to Gather

CHRISTMAS IS COMING

I wrote this little poem based on my mother's description of her childhood Christmas memories.

Grandmother cleaned the clevvy
on the kitchen wall,
scoured the porringers
of hand-turned wood,
burnished the copper bowls
to lustrous perfection.
She washed and shone
the two delph smiling cats,
polished the candlesticks
(her brassware pride and joy),
folded and cut in fancy frills
old pages of the *Clare Champion*
to trim the clevvy shelves
and then, with satisfaction,
replaced her gleaming store.
Grandmother washed the curtains
to lacey cotton crispness
so white and fresh as May.
Placed on each window sill
a holly berried turnip
with candles red
to light the Christ child's way.
But on the night
the rosary had one more trimming,
'God send Ciss and Dan and Pat and Fan
home safe next Thursday',
my mother, youngest
of that long-tailed brood,
was certain sure
Christmas had come.

– Mamo McDonald, Clones Guild, Monaghan

Hospitality & Homecomings

The preparations of November plant the seeds for the Christmas season to take root, but it is in the month of December that the magic begins to bloom. As the month progresses, the excitement builds. The Christian season of Advent – those four Sundays preceding Christmas itself, which celebrates the birth of Christ and the arrival of Christianity – has always been a particularly special time throughout Ireland, and not just because the Christian faith and Church were so much part of the social fabric here. This time of symbolic journeys, arrivals and family gatherings is particularly resonant for a country like Ireland, where so many of our sons and daughters and brothers and sisters have and still do live overseas. For many, Christmas is a joyous time of homecomings. For others, it's a time of remembrance of absent loved ones. But there is not a home in Ireland where Christmas is not a time for gathering around you those you love and marking the passing of another year.

As the darkest time of year, this is a time for bringing a little extra light into our lives, so no wonder we love to gather around blazing fires, or light a candle at the window, or illuminate our homes with twinkling fairy lights. Some homes take this to an extreme, and the old childhood pastime of counting the Christmas trees popping up in neighbouring houses has turned into a new sport of taking a drive to inspect particularly dramatic house lighting. Many department stores have been famed through the years for their decorative and magical Christmas windows, giving the phrase 'window shopping' an altogether seasonal twist.

It's a busy time, with much to do and much to gather – whether the gifts to be wrapped or the holly and ivy to be strewn about the house – but so much of that gathering is a pleasure in itself.

> Houses are but walls and beams.
> Homes are built of love and dreams.
>
> – Anonymous

A TOWNIE CHRISTMAS

"Christmas starts for me when Ronan Collins begins to play different renditions of 'O Holy Night' on his radio programme. This starts on 8 December and not before. When I was a child in the early 1960s, 8 December was a holy day, which meant a day off school. On return to school we were kept busy learning Christmas carols and the story of the Christ child. We were taught how to make paper chains (no self-respecting home would be without them) and cribs from shoe boxes. Little red, gold and silver bells were made from whatever milk bottle tops the little early birds hadn't got to first.

We were known to take the long way home from school at this time of year, to enjoy the beautifully decorated shop windows. Wellworth's department store in the town centre acted like a magnet to small children. The windows and toy department were filled with every conceivable toy. If Santa's elves were overworked he could always rely on Wellworth's for back-up and support.

On the edge of town was the Egg Store. During autumn we had gathered blackberries and sold them here. At Christmas it was quite a different place. Terrified, we ran quickly past row after row of turkeys hanging upside down. They had been reared for the Christmas market by farmers' wives who had brought them in from the country to be sold in the town.

Christmas trees began to appear in sitting-room windows, as did the bright golden star lit by an ordinary light bulb. Santa's visit to the town was eagerly awaited. The firemen and council staff had always organised everything down to the smallest detail. The crowds would gather and the lights of the towering Christmas tree would be switched on. Then we knew Santa was on his way. He would arrive in his horse-drawn sleigh (in later years it would be a fire engine and eventually a helicopter) to greet the many hundreds of parents and children in the courthouse. A small gift was given to every child. From mid-December to mid-January the church bells rang out traditional Christmas carols during daytime: 'O Come All Ye Faithful', and 'Hark! The Herald Angels Sing'. This tradition still continues to this day."

– Geraldine O'Connor, Clones Guild, Monaghan

Deck the Halls

Alongside our primal desire to introduce some festive light into these darkest of months, this is also a time when we are drawn to reconnect with nature by bringing the outside in. The use of evergreens at this darkest time of year, which has ancient associations with the winter solstice, can be as simple as trailing some greenery along your outer railings and arranging it along mantelpieces and above door frames inside the house, or as elaborate as making your own wreaths for doorways and arrangements of foliage throughout the house.

"Every Christmas week a few friends and I travel out to the local bog and cut some attractively shaped branches from pine trees and from berried holly bushes. We take them to my home, where we lay each pine branch on a workspace, trimming it if necessary. Then we attach a piece of berried holly, securing in place with twine, and arrange them together with a few red ribbons, pine cones and poinsettias to make pretty Christmas decorations. Sometimes we spray with snow or silver frosting. We place one under each stained glass window. They help brighten up our chapel for Christmas and are a cheaper alternative to the traditional Christmas wreath."

– Winnie McCarron, Ballinode Guild, Monaghan

Holly and ivy have long been traditional favourites in Ireland. Holly was especially prized for its bright red berries, but this most symbolic of evergreens has long been used to signify eternal life. Holly flourishes in midwinter, which historically gave even the poorest of people ample means with which to decorate their homes. In ancient times it was thought to be a deterrent to witches and thus considered a sign of good luck. Ivy was also believed to bring good luck, particularly if it grew up the walls of a house to protect the occupants from harm and from evil spirits. Its long tendrils allow it to be festooned about the house in a festive manner. Moss was also collected by children for decorating the crib that every home would traditionally have at Christmas time.

There are various superstitions relating to bringing foliage in and out of the home. Some say that if the holly is the first evergreen to be brought indoors, the man of the house will get the upper hand for the year to follow, leading some women to instruct their children to bring the ivy first. And it was unlucky to discard the holly and ivy before Twelfth Night, or 'Little Christmas', as 6 January is known in Ireland. Throwing away a symbol of good fortune was considered to be asking for trouble!

Mistletoe is associated with fertility goddesses, in Nordic mythology at least. But unlike the prolific holly and ivy, mistletoe was very rare in Ireland, despite Edwardian attempts to introduce it from Britain, where it is native. Thankfully there are many other kinds of evergreen foliage to choose from, and you'll often have to look no further than your own garden.

"Using natural elements from your garden can be a decorative and cheap way to light up the mantelpiece. Cut small branches of the larch tree with the acorns on it and dry them out before spraying with gold or silver spray. Then arrange them on the mantelpiece with some bigger acorns, and place some holly berries in between the branches. Last, intertwine red berry lights on the branches and holly. (If there isn't a plug socket near the mantelpiece you could use battery-operated lights.)"

– Breda O'Donnell, Scariff Guild, Clare

Christmas Cracker Arrangement

MARY O'GORMAN, MAYNOOTH GUILD, KILDARE

This is a simple but effective arrangement. I have made it with an empty Pringles container and used a pencil for the dowel, which is the peg to hold it in place and stop it rolling off the mantelpiece.

What you'll need

- 1 hard cardboard tube
- measuring tape or ruler
- craft knife
- 1 piece of dowel, roughly 5cm (2in) long
- PVA glue, or glue gun
- red or gold wrapping paper
- Sellotape
- 1 piece of dry Oasis foam
- ribbon
- scissors
- selection of artificial flowers, holly and Christmas picks
- silver or gold metallic spray (or use fake foliage)

Optional extras

- candle
- fake robin

1. Wash and dry the cardboard tube, if necessary. Measure the tube and mark out an opening in the centre of it, measuring 6cm x 5cm (2½in x 2in).

2. Carefully cut out the opening with a craft knife. Cut the dowel (or pencil) into two 2.5cm (1in) pieces and glue them lengthways to the bottom of the tube to stabilise it. If you are using tacky PVA glue, you'll need to set it aside to dry. The dowel may slip about until it is set, but it can be re-adjusted as the glue dries.

3. Cut out a length of wrapping paper 36cm x 60cm (14½ in x 24in).

4. Starting between the two dowels, cover the tube with the wrapping paper, securing with Sellotape. Twist the ends of the paper like a Christmas cracker to hold in place, and tie a piece of ribbon to fasten each side.

5. Cut through the paper at the opening you made, piercing a hole in the centre of the paper and then cutting out to each corner to give four triangular pieces. Fold each of these triangles back into the tube so that they are tucked away.

6. From the Oasis foam cut a piece 6cm x 5cm x 7.5cm (2½ in x 2in x 3in). Squeeze some glue onto the inside base of the tube and insert the Oasis directly onto the glue. Leave to dry.

7. Arrange the flowers and Christmas picks, pushing the stems into the Oasis.

8. If you are using a candle, insert it into the middle of the Oasis foam first and then add the flowers and fake robin, if using.

Christmas Wreaths

Does anything say 'Christmas' quite like a wreath hanging on a hall door? There are some beautiful wreaths available to buy, but once you master the basic technique, you'll be amazed at how versatile homemade wreaths can be. You can use a wire base if you like, but garden prunings from shrubs and small trees can be used instead: willow, dogwood and hornbeam are all suitable. Whatever branches you do use need to be about the thickness of a pencil and pliable enough to weave into a wreath – to test them, if you can twist them around your wrist without the branches splitting, then you're in business.

Twist your chosen material into a circular shape, securing with wire and adding more volume until you have a wreath that is ready for decoration. Consider whether you wish to hang your wreath indoors or outdoors: hardier evergreens are suitable for outdoor wreaths, while dried berries can look beautiful on an indoor wreath, as can dried flowers such as pink and blue hydrangea and purple teasels. If these are very faded, consider spraying them silver or gold before adding them to the arrangement.

Wreaths can also make gorgeous Christmas gifts – consider making aromatic kitchen wreaths from cinnamon sticks, cloves and dried orange slices. Raffia is an affordable and hardy addition to wreaths: try stringing a piece of pliable wire with fresh cranberries and weaving some raffia through the berries before arranging the wire in your wreath.

Or pick up a string of battery-operated fairy lights, which are available in various shapes and colours, and weave this through. This is especially effective on glass doorways so that the lights are reflected both inside and out.

“*I don't use a lot of commercial decorations as I prefer to use greenery from the garden – holly, ivy, rosemary, hebe and branches of Japanese larch are particularly lovely. Some years ago a friend gave me a wreath made from ivy branches. I duly decorated it and when the season was finished I hung it in an outdoor shed. Imagine my surprise when I took it down the following Christmas and it had a perfect little bird's nest built into it. For many years we treasured it greatly. We always hung it outside but unfortunately a storm blew up one night and we found it in the garden minus its nest. I hung it again, but sadly the birds didn't oblige me a second time around!*”

– Eily Kennedy, Annascaul Guild, Kerry

UNPACKING THE CHRISTMAS

"The day before Christmas Eve was a special, magical day for us. Mammy and Daddy took the pony and went to town to bring home 'the Christmas'. Mammy would say, 'The house has to be cleaned and decorated before we come back.' We were so excited thinking of the lovely things that they would buy, but we also had a great adventure that day. It was the job of the children to go to the woods or the laneways and bring home the holly and the ivy. Off we went, and sometimes there was a light snow or frost. To look up into the trees and the sun glistening on them, red berries hanging down in bunches – it was like being in another world, the air crisp and clear, and the fields so beautiful, tipped with white like an American Christmas card.

We would drag home as much as we could carry and decorate the dresser with holly entwined with the ivy, putting a good bunch behind every picture. Then the lamps had to be cleaned, one for the wall in the kitchen and the other for the table in the parlour. The delicate globes had to be washed very carefully with suds and warm water and dried with newspaper.

When Mammy and Daddy came home, 'the Christmas' was unpacked. There was the ordinary shopping – the tea, the sugar, the flour – but also fruit biscuits, sweets, jelly and packet custard, minerals for us and a jar of porter (our own big brown crock jar refilled and corked in the pub for two and six) for the visitors, and maybe a little bottle of sherry for the ladies. Ladies did not typically drink in those times, but they took a sherry at Christmas.

The lamp was lit in the kitchen, the decorations were up, and we were ready for Christmas Eve. The excitement was at fever pitch, as we danced around the house, happy that we were all together."

– Maura Kenny, Moore Guild, Roscommon

Holiday Bouquet

MAIREAD O'GORMAN, CAMROSS GUILD, WEXFORD

If looked after properly and refreshed every week, this festive bouquet can last you right through the holidays.

What you'll need

- fresh flowers and/or greenery with red berries
- pair of garden pruning shears
- glass urn or vase
- packet of cranberries (quantity will depend on the size of your urn or vase)
- jug of water

1. Remove the foliage from the lower stems of your flower stems and greenery (leaves left in water promote decay). Snip off about half an inch from the end of each stem and splice the stems of any flowers to encourage absorption of water.

2. Partially fill the urn or vase with cranberries and use these to help arrange flowers and greenery at different angles and heights. Fill the container to just below the rim with the rest of the berries.

3. Slowly and carefully fill the container with water. The fresh flowers will last about a week but the cranberries will stay fresh for about three weeks. To keep the berries looking fresh and clean, change the water every week, when you can also replace the fading flowers with fresh ones.

ICA Tip

Should you be given a Christmas flower arrangement, don't dispose of it once the fresh flowers have faded. As long as you keep the Oasis foam watered, the greenery or evergreen material should last for weeks. Simply remove the dead flowers, taking note of where they were placed in the Oasis, and then carefully replace with fresh flowers of a similar shape and stem length. This will give you a lovely arrangement that will last well into the New Year.

Choosing your Christmas Tree

Choosing the right Christmas tree is a serious matter, and one in which many considerations must be balanced: you don't want the tree to dwarf the room, or vice versa. Do you love the smell of a tree in the room, and if so, are you prepared to put up with it shedding needles? Whatever tree you choose – short or tall, fat or skinny – the fun starts as you unpack the box of family decorations collected over the years, and get the season properly under way.

The tradition of the Christmas tree has strong links with northern Europe, and Germany in particular, where an eighth-century saint by the name of Boniface reputedly cut down a sacred oak that was to be used as an altar for the sacrifice of a young boy. A young fir tree sprang up where the oak had been and St Boniface embraced this new tree as a symbol of his Christian faith.

The first known example of a tree being brought indoors also took place in Germany, when the reformist Martin Luther illuminated a tree with candles to remind children of the light that Jesus Christ brought to the world. Within a century or two, fir trees were being decorated at Christmas with fruits, nuts, sweets and paper flowers.

The Christmas tree was not introduced to Britain and Ireland until Victorian times, when the German-born Prince Albert introduced the tradition of a lighted tree to Windsor Castle. The fashion caught on in wealthy circles, as fashions tend to, and fashion quickly became tradition.

Of course, not everyone wants the bother of a traditional Christmas tree, so why not just bring in a sally branch and decorate it instead?

MARY'S CHRISTMAS BRANCH

"A few years ago I attended a demonstration on Christmas arrangements and decorations in our beautiful florist's shop here in Carraroe, County Sligo. The following summer when I was getting some work done in the garden, I thought to set aside a branch and decorate it for Christmas. I kept it simple, putting the branch in a bucket of sand and covering the bucket with red satin material (from an old skirt from my daughter's room). I sprayed the branches silver, hung red baubles on all the main branches and put on plain Christmas lights. That was it.

I placed it in my sunroom and it just shone – so simple yet it lit up the room. I gave my friends similar branches the following year, and so it has become a trend around Sligo now! It costs so little and looks so good. It is those things we make ourselves that give us the most pleasure. I can reuse it from year to year. We love it."

– Mary Harkin, Lakeview Guild, Sligo

VIEWS.
PARI
AND ITS ENVI
TOMMY 93
AN DREAM CITY
THE SPEC
BERGERE

Festive Decorations

Why not get everyone, from grandchildren up to granddad, to help prepare for Christmas? It helps to keep small people busy and out of trouble, and they can be given very important jobs to do leading up to the festive season. Cereal boxes, cardboard, paint, glitter, string can be used – with a bit of imagination – to make beautiful decorations to treasure for years to come.

When it comes to decorating the house, store each room's decorations in individual boxes (e.g. sitting room, hall, kitchen, etc.). This way you can decorate each room at your leisure and cut back on clutter by not having to search through box after box for that favourite ornament, or wonder which room it should go in. Ensure that boxes are of a manageable weight, shape and size – and don't forget to label them clearly.

If you or one of the family is particularly artistic, consider painting one or two festive cartoons on the front windows of your house with poster paint. Or pick up a few stencils and a spray can of fake snow from your local craft shop and use them to create pretty patterns on your windows, perhaps around a display of the classic Christmas candle for which Ireland is so famed.

“*I was a child of the 50s and early 60s and the fourth child of a family of eight. Christmas in our house was brilliant, what with all the preparations – getting the holly and putting up the paper decorations, in all different colours and patterns, that you bought in the hardware shop. We would hang them on the kitchen ceiling along with balloons of every shape and size.*”

– Eilish McDonnell, Horseleap Streamstown Guild, Westmeath

Up-cycled Christmas Decorations

JOE (JOSEPHINE) KEANE, WEXFORD TOWN GUILD, WEXFORD

As well as the work I do promoting local ICA activities, I'm also a tutor for sewing and craft classes. I particularly love to up-cycle clothes and other items. For this project I took an old music book and transformed the score into Christmas decorations. Made with love, a set of six of these make lovely Christmas presents for family, neighbours and friends. They can be displayed in an attractively shaped box, which you can cover with Christmas paper. This is a lovely crafts project to complete with children or grandchildren.

What you'll need

- template of your shape(s) of choice, e.g. heart, star, etc.
- an old music book
- red embroidery thread
- filling, to stuff your shapes

1. Use the template to mark your desired shapes on the music scores. Cut out as many shapes as you need. You will need to cut out both a front and a back for each decoration.

2. For each decoration, place the front and back together. With the red thread, begin embroidering a running stitch halfway around the edge, stitching the two together.

3. Carefully stuff with filling, taking care with the music sheet as it can easily crease or tear.

4. Once the decoration is stuffed to the desired capacity, continue to sew the rest of the way around the shape, ensuring that the filling is encased. Finish off neatly.

Pine Cone Christmas Decoration

DEBRA DUNNE, SWORDS GUILD, DUBLIN

As a craft promoter and aspiring craft teacher, I love to make quirky 'quilted' fabric Christmas decorations. They are relatively simple to make, look great on the tree (see page 202 for photo) and make a lovely gift. This pine cone decoration takes about an hour to make.

What you'll need for each pine cone:

- 7cm Styrofoam egg (available in craft shops)
- 18 x 5cm (2in) squares of green fabric
- 16 x 5cm (2in) squares of red fabric
- 70 sequin pins, approx.
- 10cm (4in) thin red ribbon, approx.
- 10cm (4in) thick green ribbon, approx.
- scissors
- sewing pins

1. Starting at the pointed end of the egg, pin a piece of green fabric so that the point of the egg is covered, secure with two pins and repeat for the top of the egg. Secure the red ribbon (for hanging) to the egg with two pins about halfway down the egg.

2. Each row contains four triangles of the same fabric, with each triangle pointing down towards the point of the egg. To make each triangle, fold a square in half diagonally ('wrong' sides together) to form a large triangle, and then fold this triangle in half again.

3. For the first row, and starting at the bottom of the egg, place a red folded triangle pointing downwards and pin it in place at the triangle's top two corners. Place a second folded triangle on the opposite side of the egg, and secure in place. Place the final two triangles between the first two, securing each with two pins. You now have one complete row of four triangles.

4. For the second row, using the same procedure, add four triangles of green fabric a little less than half an inch above the preceding row. Place each triangle so that their points are toward the dividing line of the first row. Secure each triangle with two pins as before.

5. Continue placing four triangles per row, alternating fabric each row. To finish, pin a green bow on top of the pine cone.

ICA Tip

You can adjust how much red ribbon you want to use, depending on how high or low you'd like the cone to hang.

Clones Lace Christmas Bauble

MÁIRE TREANOR, CLONES GUILD, MONAGHAN

Clones lace is an Irish crochet lace named after the town where it was marketed. When I first came to Clones in the late 1980s I was introduced to the heritage of the local crochet lace by Mamo MacDonald, a vibrant personality, women's rights activist and former ICA National President (1982–1985). I have been researching and teaching Clones lace and Irish crochet lace since then. This is the first (and less ambitious) of two of my original designs.

What you'll need

- mercerised thread, no. 10 or 20
- crochet hook, no. 1.50 or 1.25
- scissors
- a coloured Christmas bauble

Abbreviations

- ch = chain
- ck = Clones knot
- dc = double crochet stitch
- p = picot
- sc = single crochet stitch
- skn = slip knot
- ss = slip stitch
- st = stitch
- tr = treble

Tension

If you find that these directions don't work for you, improvise. Your tension might be tighter or looser. Don't worry about this. It is hand work and everybody's tension is different.

1. Row 1: 6 ch, ss to 1st ch to make circle.
2. Row 2: 10 dc into circle, ss to close.
3. Row 3: 4 ch loop, ss through tops of 2nd dc of previous row, repeat row 2 five times – 6 loops.
4. Row 4: 2 loops into every 2nd loop of previous row – 9 loops.
5. Row 5: work 9 loops, repeat for 4 rows, adding a loop when you feel it is necessary to keep the circle flat. Check that the coloured bauble fits inside the crocheted cover.
6. Row 9: increase to 5 ch loops.
7. Rows 11–12: increase to 6 ch loops.
8. Row 13: 4 ch, ck 4 ch, ss to loop of previous row, 6 rows of cks.
9. Row 20: 4 ch, ss to previous row, as in row 3. At this stage, put your coloured bauble into the centre of the crocheted cover.
10. Row 21: Decrease to 3 loops.
11. Row 22: Use your own initiative at this stage, but you can probably decrease to 2 ch loops and then miss loops to finish off. You can work around the original gold-coloured top, or make your own top. Finish off.
12. To add a long loop, crochet about 40 ch, ss into the 1st ch and finish off.

Clones Lace Angel

MÁIRE TREANOR, CLONES GUILD, MONAGHAN

I have been researching Clones lace and Irish crochet lace since the late 1980s, as well as attending workshops in the USA a couple of times each year, and writing articles and designing patterns for publication. I run workshops on Christmas decorations in Clones lace and this is one of the most popular of my original patterns (see page 85 for photo).

What you'll need

- crochet hook, no. 1.50, 1.25 or 0.60
- mercerised white thread, no. 10, 20 or 60
- PVA glue
- scissors

Abbreviations

- ch = chain
- ck = Clones knot
- dc = double crochet stitch
- sc = single crochet stitch
- ss = slip stitch
- st = stitch
- tr = treble

Tension

Remember that Irish crochet is the original freeform crochet and this pattern is meant as a guide. Everybody's tension is different, so you should improvise if necessary. Be sure not to cut the thread until the angel is complete.

For the head

1. Ch 5 ss into first stitch to make a circle.
2. Row 1: 8 dc (sc) into circle.
3. Rows 2–4: dc (sc) 2 into each dc of previous row.
4. Rows 5 and 6: dcs (sc) into every stitch. Every 4th dc, miss one dc.
5. Rows 7–9: dc into every dc of previous row.
6. Row 10: put a small ball of cotton wool into the centre and start decreasing the head.
7. Continue for rows 11 and 12.
8. When head is covered, ss to close.

For the bodice

1. Row 1: *Crochet 4 ch. ss to head.* Repeat 3 times.
2. Row 2: Crochet 4 dc into loop of previous row.
3. Rows 3–4: Crochet 2 dc into each dc of previous row, to make circle.
4. Rows 5–6: Crochet dc into each dc of previous row, keeping circular shape.

For wing 1

1. Ch 4 ss into 2nd dc of previous row. Repeat crocheting 9–10 loops.
2. 2 ch ss into loop of previous row. Continue with 4 ch loops and ss to previous row to end (8–9 loops).
3. Continue until 2 loops remain. Make 5 ch on last row.
4. Ss and ch down right side of wing.
5. To edge wing: turn. *ck. 3 dc into outside row of loop. ck* Repeat * to * to top of wing (7–8 ck).
6. Continue * to * down left-hand side.
7. 5–6 ss into dcs along front of bodice.

For wing 2

1. To measure the placing of the second wing, fold the bodice in half and gauge where to start wing 2.
2. Repeat stages for wing 1.

For the skirt

1. To close wings, fold wing and make 3 ch from last ck to 1st ck.
2. *Crochet 2 x 4 ch loops under wing. Ss into 2nd dc on bodice.* Repeat * to * to 2nd wing (4–5 ch loops).
3. 3 ch from 1st ck of wing to last ck. Repeat stage 20.
4. Crochet 3 ch loops under each wing (16 loops).
5. Continue crochet loops for 12 rows.
6. Next row: 4 ch. Ck. 4 ch ss into loop. Repeat all round loops.
7. Repeat this row. Finish off.

For the halo

1. Make buttony. Or 5 ch ss last st to first st to make circle.
2. 10 dc into circle.
3. 5 ch (1st 2 ch like tr). * Tr into double tops of 2nd dc of previous row. 3 ch.*
4. Repeat stages * to * 3 more times. 3 ch. ss to 1st loop to complete circle.
5. 5 dc into each loop (6 times).
6. Ss into tops to 3rd dc of each set and make ck.
7. Then ss into tops remaining dcs in each loop.
8. To make loop with which to hang angel, crochet 20 ch or preferred length of chains.
9. Fold and ss into 1st ch.
10. Cut thread and finish off.

To finish

Dip angel into PVA glue. Pull into shape and, using plastic gloves or a plastic bag, push your finger up through the centre of the body to achieve the shape of the angel. Leave on a tray, covered with cellophane, in a hot press overnight.

MY CHRISTMAS ANGEL

"It was the winter of 1992. Christmas was just three days away but for me it might as well have been a million light years away. It was two years since my husband had passed away and I was still struggling to come to terms with it. My husband was American and we had moved to Ireland from Virginia as he thought this was a better place to raise children. We were here a little over six months when he died suddenly, leaving me with six young children – five boys and a girl – ranging in age from three to thirteen.

I had been living in a cottage in the countryside but had just moved into my new home in the town centre of Ennistymon, County Clare. Fortunately, I didn't have a mortgage hanging over my head as I had used my husband's life assurance money to get my house built. But now the place was covered with boxes waiting to be unpacked and I found myself looking around in despair. I missed my husband badly. He would have had this place sorted out in no time. I had been dependent on him for so many things. Now I had to stand on my own two feet and the transition was difficult and painful. I did not even want to celebrate Christmas: without him there was no joy in it. For my children's sake, I had to make an effort, but I was exhausted from the move.

The doorbell rang. Standing outside was a young man who introduced himself as Tom Simon from Seattle, which is where my husband came from. He explained that he knew Mary, my husband's sister, who was a Holy Names nun in Seattle. He was making a trip to Ireland and she had asked him to look in on us. I invited him in and told him he could stay with us.

Tom was just amazing. He went out and got a Christmas tree. In next to no time, he and my children had decorated the tree, hung up the stockings and put up the Christmas decorations. I had bought a turkey for Christmas, but really didn't have the heart to cook Christmas dinner. Tom insisted I sit down and relax. He wouldn't let me do a thing. He cooked the turkey with all the trimmings with the help of my older sons – the head chef assisted by the sous chefs!

I had tears in my eyes when I beheld the table overflowing with food. It looked so festive set with the best china and a centrepiece of red candles and greenery. It was the best Christmas dinner I ever had. There was juicy turkey with delicious gravy, stuffing, mashed potatoes, honey-glazed carrots, sweet potatoes, sautéed mushrooms and stir-fried broccoli with red peppers.

As we said grace, I felt my husband was looking down on us with a smile on his face, as if to say, 'You know I'll always take care of you.' My heart was full as I thanked God for sending me what I needed most at that time, this stranger – my Christmas angel."

– Aloma McKay, Ennistymon Guild, Clare

IS SANTA REAL?

'Is Santa real?' asked the little boy
Of his mother who was stirring the pot.
She looked into his quizzical eyes;
'You see, Paul told me he's not.'

'Don't you get presents every year?' she asked,
'So why are you in doubt?'
'Cos I never see him, do I.
He creeps in, then sneaks out.'

'Have you ever seen the wind
That blows the trees and whines?
No, but you can tell the power of it
By the trail it leaves behind
Of leaves blown into huddles
And branches all stripped bare.
You did not see a bit of it
But you know that it was there.

'So why can't Santa do the same
And remain a mystery?
He'll always leave the presents
Beneath the Christmas tree.'

– Peg Prendeville, Ballyhahill/Loughill Guild, Limerick

And is it true,
This most tremendous tale of all,
Seen in a stained-glass window's hue,
A Baby in an ox's stall?
The Maker of the stars and sea
Become a Child on earth for me?

– John Betjeman, from 'Christmas'

Santa's Room.
Please Knock!

Bringing Home the Christmas

Historically the *margadh mór* (big market) kick-started the countdown to Christmas in Ireland. This 'live market' was where live fowl, such as turkeys, geese and hens, were sold, and it was followed by a 'dead market' closer to Christmas, at which all sorts of things were bought and sold alongside the poultry: clothes, whiskey, sweets, tobacco, butter, farm-grown vegetables and dried fruit and nuts for the Christmas pudding. Boiled on Christmas Eve after the house had been decorated with laurel, holly and ivy, the nineteenth-century pudding bore little resemblance to the modern Christmas pudding that we now prepare weeks, if not months, before the big day.

But the tradition of 'bringing home Christmas' – stemming from a time when people would literally have gone to the market to bring home everything needed for Christmas – stayed alive in rural Ireland right up to the 1950s and 1960s.

The Feast of the Immaculate Conception on 8 December remains a day when much of rural Ireland goes to town to start the seasonal shopping, although traditionally for some, money could only be spent on 'the Christmas' once a little extra money had been earned from Christmas, and specifically from selling a bird or two at the market. For many, the last food shop would take place as close to the holidays as possible, to ensure fresh food would last.

While the local grocer may no longer present loyal customers with an annual 'Christmas box' of seasonal gifts, and the postman may not stop at every house for a festive treat, this is still a time for showing appreciation for the wider community; for cementing bonds with those we work or deal with throughout the year, whether at the office party or the book club Christmas drinks, the ICA get-together or the Twelve Pubs of Christmas with old college pals. It is in these weeks preceding the heart of Christmas that we reaffirm connections outside the home and open up our homes to those whose friendships we value.

For many Irish families, that sense of 'bringing home the Christmas' is very much alive: welcoming loved ones back to the family homestead, gathering gifts beneath the tree and fresh food for the fridge, filling your home with the sounds of family and friends having the craic, and your kitchen with smell of mince pies and mulled wine.

BRINGING THE GOOSE TO MARKET

"My childhood memories of many a happy Christmas long ago in Strokestown, Roscommon are as clear to me today as they were all those years ago. Long before the Christmas plum pudding was even made, I would be given the very important job of feeding the geese and turkeys to get them ready for the market. It was hoped they would make five shillings for a turkey, and three shillings and six for a goose. Every penny counted. When they sold, the fowl provided the Christmas money for the house. They were brought to the market where Mammy and the children would stand with them, often on cold wet days, hoping for a sale and a good price. Women worked hard in those times but God was good and they nearly always sold.

We held on to a couple of turkeys or geese – one for Christmas Day and one for New Year's Day, which was always a big feast at that time. The day before Christmas Eve, the fowl chosen for the big dinner was killed. If it was a goose, it had to be plucked while still warm, a job none of us liked because you had to be so careful not to tear the delicate skin. The shed used to look as if it was snowing, with feathers on the ground, up in the air and all over us. These were valuable and were gathered up by my mother, to make feather pillows and a new mattress if it was needed. The wings were used for cleaning the hearth. Every bit of the goose was used. When it was cleaned out, its neck and insides were boiled down with potato and onions to make a lovely soup for Christmas Eve when we came back from midnight Mass."

– Maura Kenny, Moore Guild, Roscommon

Mince Pies

NIAMH HEADON, BALLYMORE EUSTACE GUILD, KILDARE

From the time I was old enough to mash butter into flour and icing sugar with a fork, I was initiated into the sacred realms of Christmas baking. Dozens of mince pies were made every year and rapidly frozen before the rest of the family realised there were more pies than those set before them. Today I freeze batches of pastry, which takes up less space.

Makes about 8–12 pies, depending on how thin you roll the pastry

- 225g (8oz) plain flour
- 50g (2oz) icing sugar
- 140g (5oz) butter, at room temperature
- 1 egg yolk
- 1 tablespoon ice-cold water
- 1 teaspoon lemon juice

For the filling

- 1 jar mincemeat, about 400g (14oz)

To finish

- beaten egg
- caster sugar

You'll also need

- 12-cup bun tin
- pastry cutter

ICA Tip

This sweet pastry can also be made with gluten-free flour using a straight swap, although you may need to adjust the amount of liquid to achieve the desired pastry consistency.

1. Sieve the flour and icing sugar into the bowl of a food processor and add the butter, mixing it at a very low speed. In a separate bowl, beat the egg yolk, ice-cold water and lemon juice. Once the dry ingredients become like breadcrumbs, add the egg mixture and continue mixing. Once it comes together as a pastry, allow the processor to run for another five or six seconds to save on kneading, but no more.

2. Turn out onto a large piece of cling film, flatten the pastry and wrap well. Rest in the fridge for 30 minutes.

3. Preheat oven to 200°C/400°F/Gas 6. Grease the bun tin or line with paper cases.

4. Lightly flour the work surface and rolling pin. Knead the pastry a little to loosen it, then separate one-third of the pastry and set it aside.

5. Roll out the large piece of pastry to the desired thickness – I like a very thin pastry with lots of mincemeat. Cut out the pie bases with a plain pastry cutter that matches the size of a flattened paper case/bun tin hole. (If you don't have pastry cutters, a pint glass will do.) Place the pastry bases into the lined or greased tin, and fill each with mincemeat.

6. Roll out the remaining pastry, and cut out the pastry lids using a fluted cutter that matches the size of your paper cases/bun tin holes (or a smaller glass will do). Moisten the underside of each lid before setting in place. Gently push the edges down to seal. Cut two slits in the lid or prick with a fork to allow steam to escape.

7. Brush with beaten egg and sprinkle with caster sugar. Bake in preheated oven for 15–20 minutes until golden but not brown.

8. The mince pies can be frozen once fully cooled. Defrost fully before reheating. Serve on their own or with whipped cream and a hot port or mulled wine.

CHRISTMAS MEMORIES

The following is a poem I came across many years ago in Ireland's Own *magazine. I read it every year at our Guild Christmas party. You could hear a pin drop as members are transported back to their childhood Christmases of long ago.*

– Geraldine O'Connor, Clones Guild, Monaghan

I remember the smell of the raisin cake,
The odour of pudding and pie.
I remember the candles on the sill
And the stars so bright in the sky.

I remember the kitchen table scrubbed
And laden with things to eat.
I remember the heat from the fire there,
Warming my tiny feet.

I remember the holly berries
And the moment we said grace.
I remember the laughter that filled the room
And my mother's smiling face.

I remember the songs we used to sing,
My father coming from town.
I remember the peace of our little home
And the soft snow falling down.

I remember my face at the window pane
Watching the stars on high.
I remember the Christmas I thought I saw
Santa ride down from the sky.

I remember the door open for wandering feet,
The spell of the night about.
I remember how I'd run to close it,
So I wouldn't let Christmas out.

I treasure all of these little things
As memories fond and bright
Of an Irish home where God sat down
At our table on Christmas night.

– Author unknown

Mincemeat Crumble Bars

MARY HARAN, COOLANEY GUILD, SLIGO

These quick and easy bars are a useful alternative to individual mince pies, especially if you don't have any pastry prepared or have forgotten to take it out of the freezer in time. They're also a handy shape for packing into a backpack with a flask of hot tea for long, post-Christmas winter walks.

Makes 12 bars

- 400g (14oz) mincemeat

For the base

- 140g (5oz) butter, plus extra for greasing
- 85g (3oz) golden caster sugar
- 150g (5½oz) plain flour
- 85g (3oz) cornflour

For the topping

- 110g (4oz) self-raising flour
- 85g (3oz) golden caster sugar
- 85g (3oz) butter, at room temperature
- 3 tablespoons flaked almonds

To finish

- icing sugar, for dusting

You'll also need

- 20cm x 28cm (8in x 11in) shallow cake tin

1. Preheat oven to 200°C/400°F/Gas 6.
2. Grease the cake tin with butter.
3. To make the base layer, beat the butter and sugar in a large mixing bowl until light and fluffy. Sieve in the flour and cornflour and use your hands to form the mixture into a ball.
4. Push the dough into the cake tin, pressing it out and into the corners, and chill in the fridge for 20 minutes.
5. Bake the base in the preheated oven for 12–15 minutes or until puffed and golden.
6. Meanwhile, make the topping. Combine the flour and sugar in a large mixing bowl. Cut the butter into pieces, add to the bowl and rub lightly to make coarse crumbs. Stir in the flaked almonds.
7. Spread the mincemeat over the base layer and scatter over the topping. Return to the oven for a further 20 minutes or until the topping is golden.
8. Allow to cool slightly before cutting into 12 pieces. Transfer to a wire rack to cool completely. Dust lightly with icing sugar.

Mincemeat Swirls

MARY BIRNEY, MINAUN GUILD, WATERFORD

I picked up this idea from a TV cookery programme many years ago. It makes a welcome change from the traditional mince pie, which I find can sometimes be too filling. These are much lighter and they look really attractive too.

Makes about 16–20

- 175g (6oz) self-raising flour, sieved
- 25g (1oz) ground almonds
- 50g (2oz) caster sugar
- 125g (4½oz) margarine
- 1 small egg, beaten
- a little milk, if needed
- 350g (12oz) mincemeat

You'll also need

- baking parchment
- baking sheet

1. In a large mixing bowl, mix together the flour, ground almonds and sugar. Rub in the margarine. Add the beaten egg and bring together into a dough, adding a little milk if necessary.

2. Turn out onto a floured board and knead lightly. Cover and chill for at least 30 minutes or until ready to use.

3. Lightly flour some baking parchment and roll the pastry out on the paper to about 20cm x 30cm (8in x 12in).

4. Spread the mincemeat evenly over the pastry, leaving an empty margin at the end furthest away from you. Roll carefully away from you, using the baking parchment to keep the pastry intact as you roll. Dampen the margin with a little milk and continue rolling until the margin lies at the base of the roll.

5. Twist the ends of the paper. Chill in the fridge for 2 hours.

6. Preheat oven to 200°C/400°F/Gas 6. Line a baking sheet with baking parchment.

7. Remove the baking parchment from the pastry roll and cut the roll into 12mm (½ in) slices. Place on the lined baking sheet and bake in preheated oven for about 15 minutes or until golden.

8. Allow to cool slightly on the baking sheet, then move to a wire rack to cool fully.

A CHRISTMAS WINDOW

“My mother Peggy Phelan was the proud winner of Miss Cantwell’s essay-writing competition in 1929. History fails to record what exactly my mother received as her ‘handsome prize’, but I’m sure the honour and glory of having her composition printed in the local newspaper was more than enough.”
– Miriam Murphy, Blanchardstown Guild, Dublin

A WINNING WINDOW

HANDSOME PRIZES ARE OFFERED

to the pupils of St *Angela’s Academy*
By Miss Cantwell,
Liberty Square, Thurles
For the best composition on her
CHRISTMAS WINDOW

Read what these children say so truly and with such simple charm, and you will learn how to really delight the heart of a child. Prizes will be awarded in order of merit to the young authors according to the number of votes given to each by Miss Cantwell’s customers between

SATURDAY, 14TH DECEMBER AND CHRISTMAS EVE, 1929

For further particulars apply to Miss Cantwell

The great feast of Christmas is fast approaching. Already in Thurles many of the shop windows have been decorated and the most attractive of them is most certainly Miss Cantwell’s, which contains a varied selection of crackers.
The background of one of the windows is draped with black and gold brocade. Standing against it are figures and models all made of contrasting shades of crackers. When the electric lights are flashing, the different colours of these crackers are reflected in the tall mirrors at the sides and even in the glittering, golden background itself.
Many sorts of toys are on show. Here is an aeroplane ready for flight, there a sedan chair of days gone by; there are horses, chariots, windmills, sunshades, dolls, fairies, little sentries guarding frowning castles and many other attractive models, all of which are made of crackers.

The other window is draped with delicate shades of blue and rose coloured silk, which shows off to perfection the many beautifully frosted Christmas cakes and other dainties, as well as gaily coloured boxes of chocolates, which are so artistically arranged that the whole effect is suggestive of Fairyland.

At night time, when the electric bulbs of many shades are lighting up the window, you can see the rainbow colours reflected in the little pools of water in the road.

It would be impossible for anyone to pass by without standing to gaze on this beautiful scene and I should certainly advise anyone who is about to choose Christmas gifts to first pay a visit to Miss Cantwell’s and see its fairy realms behind the snow-white framework of her very attractive confectioner shop.

– Peggy Phelan (age 13 years)

Mulled Christmas Punch

CATHERINE CHARLES, AUGHAVAS GUILD, LEITRIM

It's nice to make an effort when it comes to non-alcoholic drinks, not just for children and non-drinkers, including pregnant women and designated drivers, but also to give drinkers an attractive non-alcoholic option too.

Makes 2½ litres (4½ pints)

- 1½ litres (3 pints) pure orange juice
- 2 oranges, skin pared into strips
- 3 cinnamon sticks, broken into small pieces
- 1 tablespoon ground ginger
- 570ml (1 pint) red grapefruit juice
- 1 tablespoon grenadine syrup (optional)

To serve

- 850ml (1½ pints) sparkling water

To garnish

- orange slices
- ground cinnamon (optional)

1. In a non-aluminium saucepan, combine half the orange juice with the strips of peel and the pieces of cinnamon stick. Bring to a rolling boil and simmer for 8 minutes until reduced to a third of the original volume.

2. Allow to cool a little before transferring to a large glass jug. Stir in the ground ginger and allow to cool fully before adding the remaining orange juice together with the grapefruit juice and the grenadine, if using.

3. Stir well and refrigerate until well chilled, about 2 hours.

4. Before serving, top up with sparkling water and add slices of orange and a sprinkling of ground cinnamon, if using.

ICA Tip

This recipe is also great topped up with grapefruit soda instead of sparkling water if you can find some.

Christmas Lemonade

BETTY GORMAN, CASTLETOWN GUILD, LAOIS

This was traditionally a Christmas treat when I was young, but then we started to make it in the summer for children's birthday parties. The local children loved this drink and back then it became a favourite and something to look forward to at our parties.

Makes about 1½ litres (3 pints)

- 2 lemons
- 2 oranges
- 1 grapefruit
- 25g (1oz) tartaric acid
- 50g (2oz) citric acid
- 25g (1oz) Epsom salts
- 1.8kg (4lb) sugar
- 1½ litres (3 pints) boiling water

1. Grate the zest of the oranges, lemons and grapefruit into a large non-aluminium saucepan. Squeeze in the juice of the fruit and add in the acids, Epsom salts and sugar.

2. Pour the boiling water over the fruit juice mixture and stir well for about five minutes or until all the sugar is dissolved.

3. Allow the mixture to cool, strain well and pour the strained liquid into sterilised glass bottles (see page 57) until ready to use.

ICA Tip

This lemonade has quite a strong kick to it, which is lovely, but if you prefer you can dilute it a little with plain or sparkling water.

KNOCKMANY CHRISTMAS WALK

Onwards and upwards we climb,
Through pine scented forest,
Trees proud and graceful,
With icicles as elegant pearls
Dropping to the forest floor.

Hills, glamorous in their winter coats,
Surround the chambered cairn
Where Neolithic Stone Age Man
Constructed a resting place suitable
For Queen Áine of Oriel.

Music reverberates,
The walkers celebrate,
Close to winter solstice
Each Christmas
Since the new millennium.

– Patricia Cavanagh, Ballinode Guild, Monaghan

The magic of Christmas:
Though childhood days have passed
Upon the common round of life
A Holy spell is cast.

– Author unknown

Mulled Wine

PATRICIA CAVANAGH, BALLINODE GUILD, MONAGHAN

Each year since the new millennium, on the Sunday before Christmas, my local walking club in Knockatallon on the Monaghan–Tyrone border meet up with the Clogher Valley walkers. Our annual 'mulled wine walk' takes us up to Knockmany Cairn, an ancient passage grave situated on a high hilltop. There we sing carols and share flasks of mulled wine with homemade mince pies and shortbread.

Serves 12–15

- 1 lemon, unwaxed if possible
- 1 large orange, or two mandarin oranges
- 4 dozen cloves, approx.
- 170g (6oz) brown sugar
- 2 sticks cinnamon
- 2–3 star anise (optional)
- 1 bottle red wine
- ½ bottle ruby port

To garnish

- thin slices of orange and lemon
- sprinkling of grated nutmeg (optional)

1. Pare the lemon and the orange (or mandarins) thinly and remove the pith.
2. Stud the peeled fruit all over with cloves, and add to a large saucepan with 570ml (1 pint) water. Add the brown sugar, cinnamon and star anise, if using. If you are using unwaxed lemons or oranges, you can add the peel too.
3. Stir over heat until the sugar has dissolved. Simmer for about an hour to give the flavours time to combine. (Even better, you can prepare this a day in advance to really give the flavours a chance to blend, and simply reheat it before the next step.)
4. Strain and discard the fruit and spices. Return the infused liquid to the saucepan and add the red wine and port. Reheat to bring almost to the boil.
5. Serve hot with orange and lemon slices and a sprinkling of nutmeg if desired.

THE BIG SHOP

"A big occasion in the days before Christmas was the extra big shop for the groceries. Because shops closed in the evenings and at weekends, a big shop was done to see us over the Christmas holiday and holy days – basic food and fancy extras for treats and to entertain friends and family who came to visit. All five of us couldn't go, of course, so we took turns and I loved it when my turn came to go with Mam on one of these trips.

We lived between a village and a small town and the family 'dealt with' both James Gorman's in the village and Sheridan's in the town. Making the list demanded strategy and clever planning on my mother's part because the two grocers had to be supported equally.

It was my turn and James Gorman's was our destination. Off we set in the family blue Ford Prefect car and the welcome was memorable. James himself took us into the little back room where a small table held bottles and glasses: whiskey for the men, sherry for the womenfolk and red lemonade or orange for the children, with Marietta biscuits. The health of all the family and relations who lived abroad was discussed as well as the weather and the local happenings, and then out into the shop.

I could barely see over the high counter that stretched the length of the shop but the groceries on the high shelves were easy to see. As Mam read from the list each item was taken down, placed on the counter and recorded in the duplicate book. Extra tins of fruit cocktail and jelly for the trifle. For the Christmas cake, icing sugar and ground almonds weighed out from a huge glass jar into a brown paper bag. The purchasing of these along with drinks like Fanta orange and lemonade, Afternoon Tea biscuits and Double Centre sweets filled me with anticipation and no doubt pleased the shopkeeper.

The long list of figures (£1 1s 6d for the ham, 2s 6d for a pound of butter) was added up with the little pencil James kept behind his ear, and double checked, and the bill was duly paid. And then came the ritual of presenting us with the 'Christmas box'.

The one I remember best was simply an empty Stork Margarine cardboard box neatly packed with basics like tea and sugar, tins of fruit and Goldgrain biscuits, plus a special Christmas edition of a box of 50 John Player cigarettes for Daddy and a bottle of sherry. A Christmas fruit brack sat on top in its wax wrapping decorated with a red Santa and holly.

I don't know if the size and contents of this 'Christmas box' depended on how much was spent on the day or on how much he valued the loyalty of the customer throughout the year, but it would be lifted out from under the high counter already prepared. Maybe he had others worth more or less and distributed these accordingly. The tradition of the 'Christmas box' disappeared in the late 1980s – maybe the arrival of supermarkets had an impact."

– Ada Vance, Killeshandra Guild, Cavan

Apple Cider Punch

MARION LYON, MAGHERA GUILD, CAVAN

This makes a nice alternative to mulled wine, featuring cider heated through with seasonal spices and given some extra tang with the additional fruit juices. It can be served hot or cold, depending on the occasion – and the weather!

Serves 20–25

- 1.2 litres (2 pints) apple cider
- 570ml (1 pint) cranberry juice
- 275ml (½ pint) orange juice
- 275ml (½ pint) apricot nectar (optional)
- 225g (8oz) sugar, or to taste
- 2 sticks cinnamon
- 2 star anise (optional)

To garnish

- slices of orange
- cloves

1. Combine all the ingredients in a large non-aluminium saucepan, bring just to the boil and then reduce to a low simmer for 20 minutes.

2. Serve hot poured into individual glasses garnished with orange slices studded generously with cloves. Alternatively, you could also allow the liquid to cool and transfer to a glass punch bowl, garnished with clove-studded slices of orange.

ICA Tip

When pouring hot liquid into glassware, first put a metal teaspoon into the glass or jug to absorb some of the heat and prevent the glass cracking.

SILENT NIGHT

Óiche chiúin Óiche Mhic Dé,
Cách 'na suan dís araon,
Dís is dílse faire le spéis
Naon beag naí-gheal ceananntais caomh,
Críost 'na chodhladh go séimh
Críost 'na codhladh go séimh.

"Though first written in German, in 1816, by a young priest named Father Joseph Mohr, 'Stille Nacht' has since been translated into over 140 languages, including Irish. During World War I, it was famously sung simultaneously in English and German by troops during the Christmas Truce of 1914. It was chosen as the one carol that soldiers on both sides of the front would know and love. 'Silent Night' was my mother's favourite Christmas carol and it reminds me of her when I hear it sung."

– Anne Maria Dennison, Mainistir na Féile Guild, Limerick

Silent night, Holy night,
All is calm, all is bright,
Round yon virgin mother and child
Holy infant so tender and mild,
Sleep in heavenly peace,
Sleep in heavenly peace.

Silent night, Holy night,
Son of God, love's pure light,
Radiant beams from Thy Holy face
With the dawn of Redeeming grace,
Jesus Lord at Thy birth,
Jesus Lord at Thy birth.

Silent night, Holy night,
Shepherds quake at the sight,
Glories stream from heaven afar
Heav'nly hosts sing Alleluia,
Christ the Saviour is born,
Christ the Saviour is born.

THE KERRY CHRISTMAS CAROL

Brush the floor and clean the hearth,
And set the fire to keep,
For they might visit us tonight
When all the world's asleep.

Don't blow the tall white candle out
But leave it burning bright,
So that they'll know they're welcome here
This holy Christmas night.

Leave out the bread and meat for them,
And sweet milk for the Child,
And they will bless the fire, that baked
And, too, the hands that toiled.

For Joseph will be travel-tired,
And Mary pale and wan,
And they can sleep a little while
Before they journey on.

They will be weary of the roads,
And rest will comfort them,
For it must be many a lonely mile
From here to Bethlehem.

O long the road they have to go,
The bad mile with the good,
Till the journey ends on Calvary
Beneath a cross of wood.

Leave the door upon the latch,
And set the fire to keep,
And pray they'll rest with us tonight
When all the world's asleep.

– Sigerson Clifford

“*I love the Kerry Christmas Carol. It always evokes for me a feeling of warmth and safety. It was written by Sigerson Clifford, a Cork-born poet and playwright who grew up in Cahersiveen on the Ring of Kerry, and it was published in his 1955 book of poetry,* Ballads of a Bogman.”

– Peg Prendeville, Ballyhahill/Loughill Guild, Limerick

Avocado and Roasted Almond Dip

MARGARET KYNE DOYLE, KNOCKNACARRA GUILD, GALWAY

The almond gives this avocado dip an interesting texture and an extra dimension. You can make up little individual toasts or let people dip the garlic toast 'soldiers' into the dip. Crudités, such as batons of celery or carrot, also work well, or you could serve it on little croustade bases.

Serves 8–10 as one of a selection of dips

- 140g (5oz) whole almonds, blanched
- 2–3 avocados, not overly ripe
- ¼ lemon, juice only
- pinch of salt

To serve (optional)

- 4–5 slices of your favourite bread
- 1–2 garlic cloves
- olive oil

1. Preheat oven to 180°C/350°F/Gas 4. Roast the almonds in the preheated oven for 5–10 minutes, stirring regularly. Remove from the heat and allow to cool.

2. Meanwhile, remove the skin and stone from the avocados and roughly chop the flesh.

3. Once the almonds have cooled, blend until the nuts are broken up but not ground. Add the avocado, a teaspoon or two of lemon juice and salt and blend lightly. Taste to check seasoning and add a little more lemon juice if needed.

4. If you'd like to serve with the garlic toasts, simply toast each slice of bread on one side only under a hot grill. Cut the garlic clove in half, rub the toasted side of the bread with the cut side of the garlic, and drizzle with olive oil, if using. These toasts can be cut into small squares or diamonds and topped with the avocado, or they can be cut into 'soldiers' and used for dipping.

ICA Tip

To blanch almonds, simply steep in boiling water for three or four minutes or until the skins will slip off easily.

Croustade Canapé Bases

MAURA RIORDAN, DUN LAOGHAIRE GUILD, DUBLIN

I have had this croustade recipe in a scrapbook for a number of years and find it makes a versatile base for various party nibbles. I like to use a light rye bread, which is excellent with smoked salmon and dill. They can be prepared well in advance and assembled before serving.

Makes 20 bases

- 5 slices medium-cut bread
- 110g (4oz) butter
- 1 large garlic clove, crushed
- sprig of thyme (optional)
- salt and pepper

For the filling

- 225g (8oz) smoked salmon, finely chopped
- a little lemon juice
- 3–4 tablespoons crème fraîche
- 1–2 tablespoons finely chopped dill

You'll also need

- 2 bun tins
- rolling pin
- 5cm (2in) pastry cutters
- pastry brush

ICA Tip

Other fillings that work well include a homemade chicken liver paté with a fruit chutney, some shredded spiced beef with apricot and almond chutney (see page 58) or even some avocado and almond dip (see page 108) or hot sherried crab (see page 112).

1. Preheat oven to 180°C/350°F/Gas 4 and heat both bun tins.

2. Roll each slice of bread on a chopping board with a rolling pin to make them as thin as possible. Cut out rounds of about 5cm (2in) with a plain pastry cutter.

3. In a small saucepan, melt the butter together with the garlic and thyme, if using, and a generous seasoning of salt and pepper.

4. Brush the bread rounds on both sides with the seasoned butter, popping each into a depression in the hot bun tins as you go.

5. Bake in the preheated oven for about 15 minutes or until crisp and brown. Transfer to a wire rack to cool and then store them in an airtight tin, where they will keep well for up to a fortnight.

6. Before serving, simply pile your filling into the croustades: some chopped smoked salmon in the centre, topped with lemon juice, a little crème fraîche and a scattering of finely chopped dill.

7. Arrange on a serving plate; they will keep crisp for up to three hours.

Smoked Salmon Two Ways

ANNE MARIA DENNISON, MAINISTIR NA FÉILE GUILD, LIMERICK

Smoked salmon is very versatile and a firm favourite at Christmas, when it is often used as a starter or in party canapés. These two different approaches can be used together, or you can choose whichever you prefer.

Serves 10–12 as part of a selection of canapés

For the smoked salmon paté
- 125g (4½oz) smoked salmon
- 60ml (2fl oz) crème fraîche
- 60ml (2fl oz) mayonnaise
- black pepper, to taste
- 1 tablespoon lemon juice

For the smoked salmon rolls
- 50g (2oz) cream cheese
- 2 tablespoons crème fraîche
- 1 teaspoon chopped fresh chives
- 2 limes
- 250g (9oz) smoked salmon, thinly sliced

To serve
- slices of light brown bread
- sprigs of fresh dill (optional)
- batons of carrot, celery, cucumber

You'll also need
- cling film
- tinfoil

1. To prepare the smoked salmon paté, blend all ingredients except the lemon juice in a food processor until smooth. Then add the lemon juice to taste. Transfer to a serving dish and chill until ready to serve.

2. To prepare the smoked salmon rolls, in a small bowl mix together the cream cheese, crème fraîche, chopped chives and the zest of one lime.

3. Cover a chopping board with cling film. Lay out the salmon slices in a rectangle, overlapping the slices. Spread the cream cheese mixture over the top and roll up the salmon into a sausage shape, with the cling film on the outer layer. Cover in foil and chill for at least an hour or until required.

4. When ready to serve, cut the bread into bite-sized circles (about the width of your salmon roll) and lay them out on a serving platter. Unwrap the salmon and slice to the desired thickness. Place a slice of salmon on top of each round of bread and garnish with very thin wedges of the second lime and sprigs of dill, if using.

5. Serve the dip with batons of carrots, celery and cucumber on the side.

ICA Tip

The paté can also be served as an hors d'oeuvre with toast, salad leaves and cherry tomatoes; the smoked salmon with cream cheese could be served as a canapé with pre-dinner aperitifs.

Crab Bouchées

MAIREAD O'GORMAN, CAMROSS GUILD, WEXFORD

Bouchée is simply a fancy name for 'bite', but these crab bites are certainly fancy. Prepared with large vol-au-vents, this recipe makes a lovely starter for six, but it's also perfect as smaller bites for larger numbers. It can be prepared the evening before, and kept fresh in the fridge. Simply heat through before serving.

Serves 10–12 as part of a selection of canapés

- 450g (1lb) crab meat
- 225 (8oz) mushrooms
- 50g (2oz) butter
- 2 egg yolks
- 2 tablespoons double cream
- 265ml (9fl oz) mushroom sauce (or mushroom soup)
- ½ teaspoon salt
- ½ teaspoon pepper
- ⅛ teaspoon cayenne pepper
- 150ml (¼ pint) sherry (or white wine)
- ¼ lemon, juice only

To serve

- 10–12 ready-made mini vol-au-vents
- mixed lettuce leaves
- thin slices of tomato

1. Dice the crab meat and set aside. Slice the mushrooms and sauté in a little butter for 5–6 minutes, stirring occasionally. Remove from the heat and set aside.

2. In a medium saucepan, whisk together the egg yolks and cream, add the mushroom sauce and set over a moderate heat. Stir in the prepared crab meat and mushrooms, season with salt, pepper and cayenne and cook gently for 2 minutes. Stir in the sherry or wine and a couple of teaspoons of lemon juice, or to taste, and cook for another minute.

3. At this point, you can allow to chill and refrigerate until ready to serve, and simply reheat before serving. Before serving, bake the vol-au-vents according to the instructions on the packet. Remove from the oven, allow to cool and press down the centres.

4. Spoon the warm filling into the vol-au-vents and serve garnished with mixed lettuce leaves and thinly sliced tomato.

ICA Tip

This recipe also works very well with lobster meat, and as the meat will be chopped and cooked, frozen lobster is fine to use.

"*For me, the ICA has been hugely important as it introduced me to life in the midlands when I came to live here, not knowing anyone and not having lived in Ireland for over thirty years. The ICA offered me friendship and companionship. I love the endless opportunities it offers the women of Ireland in so many different areas; it challenges me to try new crafts, to be involved in our local community, and to look further afield to similar women's organisations in the rest of the world.*

I spent a great many years living in Australia and it was never the same at Christmas (due primarily to the fact that it was summertime!) so I only got to really celebrate Christmas every two or three years.

It wasn't just the excitement and anticipation of arriving at Dublin Airport that mattered, or even the reindeer and Santa in the arrivals hall: it was when you stepped outside the airport and saw 'WELCOME HOME' in lights. Ireland is the only country that I have been to at Christmas time that welcomes home its sons and daughters in this manner. It was hugely important to all of us, as it was the real start to our Christmas celebrations.

We knew we really were home at last."

– Anne Payne, Portlaoise Guild, Laois

It's gonna take some time
But I'll get there ...

So I sing for you
Though you can't hear me
When I get through
And feel you near me
I am driving home for Christmas
Driving home for Christmas
With a thousand memories ...

– Chris Rea, from 'Driving Home for Christmas'

3

CHRISTMASTIME IN IRELAND

Words and Music by
EILISH BOLAND

Slowly

Key F

Voice

Piano

There's a house that I re - mem - ber, Where the
There's a place be - side the turf fire In a

can - dle - light will glow Just to guide the wea - ry
cor - ner warm and bright, Just to greet the wea - ry

trav - eller on his way, And the
trav - eller if he stray, And an

P. & Co. Ltd. 450

CHRISTMASTIME IN IRELAND

There's a house that I remember, where the candlelight will glow,
Just to guide the weary traveller, if he stray.
And the bells will ring out gladly from the valley down below,
For it's Christmastime in Ireland, in that land so far away.

When the misty dawn will break, on that happy Christmas morn,
And the wee ones tiptoe softly to the place where he was born.
Oh I wonder will they think of absent friends and say a prayer,
For it's Christmastime in Ireland but sure someone won't be there.

There's a place beside the turf fire in the corner of the room
Just to greet the weary traveller on his way.
And an Irish heart will welcome you by day or starry night,
For it's Christmastime in Ireland, in that land so far away.

When the misty dawn will break, on that happy Christmas morn,
And the wee ones tiptoe softly to the place where He was born.
Oh I wonder will they think of absent friends and say a prayer,
For it's Christmastime in Ireland but sure someone won't be there.

– Eilish Boland

"I have always loved 'Christmastime in Ireland', which my mother wrote over sixty years ago and which is still as poignant today. I love the image of the wee ones tiptoeing softly to the place 'where he was born'. It means so much to me as one of my sons now lives in Perth, Australia and doesn't get home too often at Christmas.

Mammy wrote this song when her two brothers were away, one in London and one at sea. My own brother went to London, and my eldest son is also in London, and so it goes. No matter what decade, there is always someone who won't make it home to Ireland for Christmas."

– Brona Ui Loing, Kilteel Guild, Kildare

Absent Loved Ones

Of course, not everyone makes it home for Christmas. The postman always played a particularly special role at this time of year in Ireland, bringing packages and parcels from all corners of the world. Children would watch out for the postman's arrival so that they could tear open parcels of goodies and read the tinsel-covered cards with news from worlds so different from theirs.

> The boys of the NYPD choir
> Still singing 'Galway Bay'
> And the bells are ringing
> Out for Christmas day ...
>
> – The Pogues, from 'Fairytale of New York'

Today, thanks to the convenience of social media and Skype, it is so much easier to keep in touch with loved ones living overseas. And today's competitively priced airline travel makes it easier for the adventurers to land on their home ground and to be reunited with family and friends just in time for the Christmas season. But somehow sending and receiving Christmas cards is still a tradition that is alive and strong.

"*My memories are going back over fifty years ago. We lived five miles outside our town. Our postman delivered the post by bicycle. Around the week before Christmas it was the custom that he was invited into most houses for his Christmas 'treat'.*

By the time he reached our house he was 'in good spirits' and knew my mother would have the Christmas pudding warming on the pan and a bottle of Guinness ready. As I was the oldest girl he would say to me, 'Bring the post and deliver it to the last four houses on the road'. I was so excited knowing that I would get a shilling or maybe a half a crown from each neighbour.

In the meantime, while I was delivering the post my mother heard all the latest news and the postman had a rest by the open fire. On my return he would give me a bar of Fry's Cream Chocolate. The postman and my mother are both long gone but the memory is as clear as if it was yesterday."

– Pauline Bligh, Lucan Guild, Dublin

Chapter 3

The Heart of Christmas:

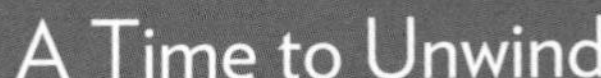

A Time to Unwind

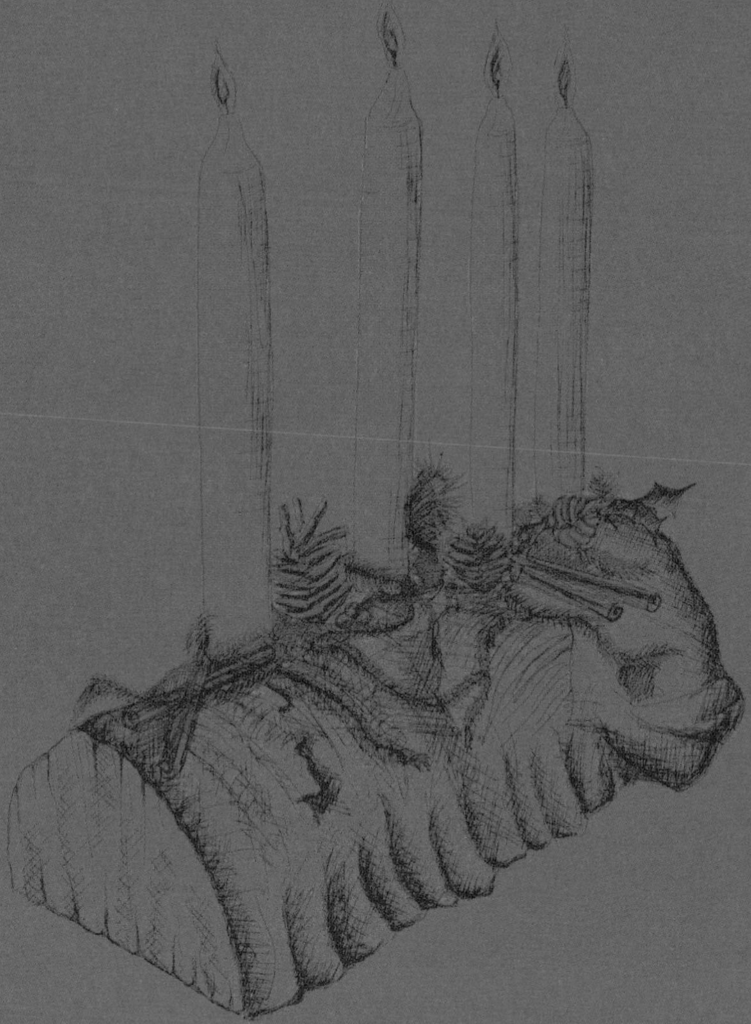

The Finishing Touches

Traditionally in Ireland, 24 December was a busy day for all the family. Many households were superstitious about decorating the house before Christmas Eve, and so all hands would be needed to deck out each room with red berries, holly, ivy, coloured crepe paper chains and streamers. And for many families, this was when the Christmas candle would be first lit – always by the youngest child in the house.

At this point you'll be glad to have kept a list of things to do in the days leading up to Christmas, and you can begin to check things off your list. You will probably want to cook your Christmas ham on Christmas Eve, and to prepare as much for tomorrow's dinner as you can: certainly the stuffing and potatoes and vegetables and giblet stock, and probably the sauces too if you can make enough storage space in your fridge. And if you haven't already done so, now is quite literally the time to put the icing on the cake.

"On the night before Christmas Eve, it was hard to sleep and morning came so fast. There was so much to do. Mammy was up with the crows building up the fire, we were never so willing to bring in the turf. The pot for the goose was scrubbed, and scrubbed to perfection until you could run a white cloth around it and take it away spotless. The big plate was taken down from the dresser, all the china gleaming in the firelight. The knives had been sharpened by the Traveller man who came to our village during the summer. The tablecloth for the parlour was starched and immaculate white.

That night in the pitch dark we all went as a family down the road with all the other dark figures –the small ones holding hands, some carrying tilly lamps or bicycle lamps – to welcome the 'baby Jesus'. Coming home in the moonlight, with the trees still like a painting, not a sound except our boots on the frosty laneway. That is something I will never forget. The lamp was lit in the parlour, and the one fire of the year set for the morning. We indulged ourselves in the Christmas soup we had made from the goose or turkey giblets, and treacle cake."

– Maura Kenny, Moore Guild, Roscommon

FROM 'CHRISTMAS EVE'

The room was decorated for Christmas. He and the children had worked all afternoon on it, with Delia running up and down from the kitchen to see how they were getting along. They had all had a great time. Even Margaret had come out of herself and made suggestions. There were swags of red and green paper chain across the ceiling, and he had put a sprig of holly behind every picture. The mistletoe was over the door going out into the hall. At one point Delia had come hurrying up to say they must save a bit of holly to stick in the Christmas pudding, and he had caught her under the mistletoe and given her a kiss. Her skin was very soft. She looked like her old self as she put her hand up against his chest and pretended to push him away. Then the children came running over and wanted to be kissed too. First he kissed them and then Delia kissed them. They were all bundled together for a minute and then the children began screaming, 'Daddy, kiss Mummy again! Daddy, kiss Mummy again!' and Delia said, 'Oh, I have to get back to the kitchen. All this play-acting isn't going to get my work done.' Lily said, 'Women's work is never done.' Lily was always coming out with something like that. You never knew what she'd say next. Margaret said, 'I want to kiss little Jesus,' and she went over to the window where the crèche was all set up, with imitation snow around it and on its roof.

The window was quite big, a bow window that bulged out into the street. Delia had filled it with her fern collection. They were mostly maidenhair ferns, some of them very tall, and she had them arranged on a table ... they made a wonderful background for the crèche, making it seem that the stable and the Holy Family and the shepherds and their animals were all enclosed and protected by a benign forest where they would always be safe and where snow could fall without making them cold. The Three Wise Men stood outside the stable as though they were just arriving. Lily had carefully sprinkled snow on their shoulders. Some of the snow had sifted down onto the carpet, where it lay glittering in the firelight.

– Maeve Brennan, *The Springs of Affection*

Brandy Butter

MARY WHITE, BARNA GUILD, GALWAY

This recipe is based on one that appeared in the Radiation Cookery Book, *first published in 1927 to introduce women to the joys and secrets of cooking on a gas hob. It is a traditional accompaniment for a steamed plum pudding, and is sometimes referred to as a 'hard sauce'.*

Serves 6–8

- 110g (4oz) butter, at room temperature
- 110g (4oz) caster sugar
- 1 tablespoon brandy or sherry
- 50g (2oz) ground almonds (optional)

1. Beat the butter and sugar to a cream, add the brandy or sherry and ground almonds, if using, and continue beating until well incorporated.
2. Pile in a dish and chill before serving with plum pudding.

Economical Almond Paste

ROSEMARY MCCARVILLE, CLONES GUILD, MONAGHAN

For some people it is the almond paste under the icing that makes a Christmas cake particularly special. But ground almonds can be expensive, so here is a clever recipe for almond paste that won't break the bank.

Makes enough to cover a 25cm (10in) cake

- 200g (7oz) ground almonds
- 200g (7oz) ground rice (or rice flour)
- 200g (7oz) caster sugar
- 200g (7oz) icing sugar, plus a little extra for dusting
- 1 large egg
- 1 teaspoon almond essence
- 1 teaspoon whiskey

To finish

- apricot jam, for brushing the cake

You'll also need

- pastry brush

1. Combine the dry ingredients in a large bowl and mix well.

2. Lightly beat the egg and stir in the almond essence and whiskey. Pour into the dry ingredients and bring together lightly with your fingers.

3. Knead lightly on a board dusted with icing sugar. Lightly dust a rolling pin with icing sugar and use it to roll out the almond paste into a circle of at least 25cm (10in) diameter.

4. To apply to the Christmas cake, loosen a teaspoon or two of apricot jam with a little hot water and use it to brush the top of the cake. Turn the cake, top down, onto the rolled circle of almond paste and press the edges to adhere before turning right way up.

ICA *Tip*

If you'd like to ice the sides of the cake as well as the top, simply double the quantities of paste and icing.

Royal Icing

MAI KELLY, MOYDOW GUILD, LONGFORD

While ready-to-roll icing is very useful for making decorative toppings such as my favourite robin redbreast (see page 127), when it comes to putting the icing on the cake, it's nice to make your own royal icing.

Makes enough to cover a 25cm (10in) cake

- 4 egg whites
- 600g (1lb 5oz) icing sugar
- 1½ teaspoons glycerine

1. Lightly whisk the egg whites in a large mixing bowl, sieving in the icing sugar little by little as you whisk. Bring to the consistency of thick peaks, which will take about 10 minutes, before folding in the glycerine and whisking a little further to integrate fully.

2. Cover the cake with a couple of teaspoons of warmed jam and then with almond paste (see page 124). Finish with a layer of icing, spread evenly with a spatula or warmed palette knife.

3. Any surplus icing can be piped onto the cake before decorating, as desired. Little silver balls and green and red ribbon can be very effective, or if you're feeling ambitious you can try your hand at the iced robin redbreast.

4. Set aside overnight to dry and allow the icing to set, and store in an airtight tin until ready to serve.

ICA Tip

If the icing on a cake goes so hard that it breaks when it's cut, you can dampen a clean cloth in cold water, wring it out and wrap the cake overnight before cutting.

Iced Robin Redbreast

MAI KELLY, MOYDOW GUILD, LONGFORD

I am in my 80s now and have been icing cakes for many years. This is one of my favourite designs, being so cheerful and festive. It looks very impressive but is straightforward enough to do, so long as you give yourself the time and space to enjoy it.

Makes one robin:

- 1 packet ready-to-roll icing, about 450g (1lb)
- food colouring, a bottle each of red, brown, orange and green

You'll also need

- greaseproof paper
- 2 very small paint brushes

1. Using a piece of greaseproof paper, draw the shape of a robin, measuring 1½ cm (4½ in) from head to tail. You could copy the robin from a Christmas card, or from an image found online. Cut out the shape so that you have a paper pattern.

2. Break or cut off a small matchbox-sized piece of ready-to-roll icing and roll it out to ½cm (¼in) thick.

3. Place the cut-out pattern of the robin over the icing and use the point of a sharp knife to cut the icing away from the pattern.

4. Paint the back and wing and the top of the head with the brown food colouring. Then paint the lower part of the head and breast with the orange colouring. Finally, lightly paint the bottom of the breast and underneath the wing with dabs of brown colouring.

5. Roll a small amount of the icing into the shape of a cigarette and paint it brown for the twig. Make small holly leaves and paint them green. Make very small balls for holly berries and paint them red.

6. Place the robin in the centre of the iced cake, and arrange the green leaves and holly berries all around the robin in a circle.

JIMÍN AGUS AN GANDAL

"One story that always stirs my recollections of Christmas long ago is from Jimín, written by Pádraig Ó Siochfhradha (An Seabhach) in the early 1900s. Jimín was used as a text book in schools for many years. The particular story that I retell here has appeared in modern Irish text books as the story entitled 'Jimín agus an Gandal', but my telling is translated loosely from the original Irish version. Jimín is a boy typical of his time who gets himself into many a scrape, especially with his mother. He gives an honest account of what went on in his house at Christmas:

A few days before Christmas, Jimín's mam and dad went to town with the horse and cart. His mother had a goose for the doctor and another for the bank man. Jimín was left with his sister Cáit to collect holly and decorate the house. Being a bit over-enthusiastic with the hammer and nails putting up the holly, he managed to knock the odd lump out of the plaster. Still, he thought the place looked cheerful and that he had done a great job. His mam wasn't a bit impressed when she came home, however, so he had to make himself scarce. He didn't see what she had brought from town, but Cáit told him there was sugar, tea, a currant cake, raisins, apples, red candles and one bottle with yellow drink, one with dark purple drink and a big jug of black stuff.

On Christmas Eve Jimín's mam killed a goose and a duck, and hung them up behind the door. Himself and Cáit made a hole in a turnip and put one of the red candles in it. That night they had a big feast of fish and potatoes, but Jimín was more interested in the sweet stuff that he knew was still in the cupboards. The neighbours called in and were given a drink from the big jug or the yellow bottle. His mam herself even had a drink of the purple stuff. When no one was looking Jimín took a slug from the big jug but had to run out the door to spit it out.

On Christmas morning his mam and Cáit went to first Mass and while his father was out milking, Jimín searched the cupboards. He filled his pockets with raisins, and took a big hunk of the currant cake. He poured a half cup of the yellow drink, but it was worse than the black stuff. He couldn't pour it back, so he called the dog, but he only sniffed it. The big gander was at the door so he got a bit of yellow meal and poured the drink over it. Sure enough the gander gulped it down. He noticed nothing for a while but then the gander started goggling, then began to walk around in circles, with his head to one side. Then didn't he spread his legs and drop his head on the ground without a gig out of him.

Jimín would be in big bother if anything happened the gander. He heard his father coming so he busied himself sweeping the floor. 'In ainm Dé,' says his dad, 'what did you do to the gander, Jimín?' It being Christmas morning, he was afraid to tell a lie so in small bits Jimín told the whole story to his dad. He was sure his mam would have to be told, so he prayed all during Mass that the Lord would save him from what was ahead of him.

When they came home the gander was beside the fire and looking himself again. His mam asked who had called to the house while she was out, as there was whiskey gone out of the bottle. But his dad winked at Jimín, and she never heard the real story."

– Peggy Lynch, Drumshanbo Guild, Leitrim

"*It was a bitterly cold night when the baby Jesus was born, with just a small fire burning in the stable where Mary and Joseph had been forced to take shelter. That night, a small brown bird flew into the stable, so plain that nobody noticed her. The bird perched awhile on a beam and then flew down to gently fan the flames with her wings. Sure enough the fire grew stronger. All through that cold night the little bird worked the flames with its wings, keeping the stable cosy and warm for the whole family. By morning, the glowing heat had turned her breast feathers to a rich flame colour. To this day, descendants of that little bird are proud of their beautifully coloured feathers.*"

– Patricia O'Toole, Newbridge Guild, Kildare

Apple Baked Ham

MAURA RIORDAN, DUN LAOGHAIRE GUILD, DUBLIN

I picked up this recipe for apple baked ham from a women's magazine back in the early 1990s and it has been a favourite ever since. It makes a nice alternative to a traditional honey-baked ham.

Serves 6–8 or more as part of a large meal

- 2.75kg (6lb) joint of ham
- 570ml (1 pint) apple juice
- 1 cinnamon stick, bruised
- 2–3 tablespoons stale white breadcrumbs
- 2–3 tablespoons soft light brown sugar
- 1–2 teaspoons dried mustard
- 25–30 cloves

To garnish

- apple slices

You'll also need

- roasting tin
- trivet
- tinfoil

1. Preheat the oven to 190°C/375°F/Gas 5.

2. Rinse the joint under cold running water, then pat dry with kitchen towel. Place on a trivet in a roasting tin and pour apple juice over. Add the cinnamon stick, cover with foil, and cook in the oven for 1½–2 hours.

3. Remove from the oven and, when cool enough to handle, cut away the skin and any underlying fat. Mix together the breadcrumbs, sugar and mustard and spread this evenly over the ham. Stud the surface with cloves.

4. Return to the oven and cook uncovered for a further 15–20 minutes or until the coating is crisp.

ICA Tip

If garnishing with fresh apple, toss the slices in a little acidulated water to prevent oxidisation and browning – a little lemon juice and water will do it. Or you could buy dried apple slices for garnishing.

Cumberland Sauce

ANNE MARIA DENNISON, MAINISTIR NA FÉILE GUILD, LIMERICK

This pouring sauce is a lovely accompaniment for a Christmas ham but it also makes a nice alternative to cranberry sauce. It is very quick and easy to make, but if you prefer to be organised, it can be made in advance and stored until ready to use.

Makes about 375ml (12fl oz)

- 225g (½lb) redcurrant jelly
- 150ml (¼ pint) port
- 1 orange, zest and juice
- 1 tablespoon mustard powder
- salt and pepper

1. Combine the redcurrant jelly, port, orange juice and zest in a small saucepan. Bring to the boil and reduce to simmer for a few minutes.

2. Blend the mustard powder with a tablespoon of water and stir this into the sauce.

3. Season with salt and pepper and simmer for 3 minutes, taking care not to boil.

4. If making in advance, transfer to a sterilised jar (see page 57), cover and refrigerate until required. Use within 2–3 weeks and serve cold.

Laying the Table

If you have the space to do so, it's a great idea to set the dining table on Christmas Eve, and not only because it is one less job to do the next day. It also looks so pretty, with sparkling glassware and cutlery, candles ready for lighting and, of course, the magical crackers, which are always fun no matter how bad the jokes! And seeing the table ready helps to fan the building anticipation for the big meal itself.

You might like to include a small flower arrangement, but even a clever use of berries such as fresh cranberries can really set the mood. You could keep it as simple as piling them up around a thick church candle set on a pretty saucer, or you could make something more elaborate by stringing them onto jewellery wire and weaving raffia around the berries. You can add in other colours or embellishments as the mood takes you. The wire can then be moulded into whatever shape you like – perhaps twisted around the candle or as part of a more elaborate table arrangement.

There are many ways to cheer up a table setting. If you have a crowd coming, taking a little time with place name tags is a lovely way to make people feel special. You can pick up brightly coloured luggage tags, and write the names in coloured pens, and maybe attach these to the Christmas crackers. With a little planning, you can make very effective festive-coloured napkin holders out of felt (see page 135). Or cut little Christmas stocking shapes out of felt, and use different-coloured thread to stitch them together in pairs to make cutlery holder pouches, which you can then decorate with sequins or pom-poms. Even running a few lengths of ribbon parallel to each other along the middle of a crisp white tablecloth can be enough to add festive cheer to a simple table setting.

Pattern

Napkin Holder

Pattern not to scale.

Poinsettia Napkin Holders

BRIDGID KEANE, ARDMORE GRANGE GUILD, WATERFORD

This could be a nice little last-minute project to delegate to a young pair of 'crafty' hands. Once you have the materials sourced and the patterns sketched out to scale, the napkin holders are surprisingly simple to prepare and assemble and they look very effective (see page 204 for photo).

What you'll need

- green felt
- red felt
- paper, to trace out pattern
- scissors

1. To make each napkin holder, trace and cut the green shape from the pattern to a length of 26cm (10½in) and a width of 7.5cm (3in). Fold in half and cut diagonally from 2.5cm (1in) along the inner fold to the outer edges, so that when you unfold the felt you have two pointed edges.

2. Make two 3.5cm (1½ in) slits as indicated on the pattern. These should be 1cm (½in) in from one length of the green, and alternately 5cm (2in) and 7.5cm (3in) from either end of the green strip.

3. Fold over, aligning the two slits so that there is a 2.5cm (1in) offset of one side of green showing under the other.

4. Cut 2 pieces of red from the pattern to a length of 12cm (5in) and width of 6cm (2½in) on the narrower side and about 6.5cm (2¾ in) on the wider side. Fold in half and cut diagonally from 2.54cm (1in) along the inner fold to the outer edges, so that when you unfold the felt you have two pointed edges.

5. Make a 3.5cm (1½in) slit in one piece as indicated, to sit 1cm (½in) in from each edge.

6. Place the slit red piece over the green, aligning the red slit just above the green slit so that you can pull the outer green strip or loop through the red slit.

7. Pass the second red piece through the green loop and adjust the petals.

CHRISTMAS EVE SWEET TEA

"*In 'Old God's time' Christmas Eve was a day of abstinence so people had fish or eggs for dinner with vegetables and potatoes. Dried salted ling was very popular, cooked in milk and onions to make a white sauce served with potatoes.*

We looked forward to our special tea on Christmas Eve after the candles had been lit. Mom would put on the new oilcloth tablecloth (the white damask one would be kept clean for Christmas Day). We children would set the table with her best china tea-set, which was only used for very special occasions. It was a sweet tea, with a huge barm brack, seed loaf, butter loaf, blackcurrant jam and Mom's delicious fruit and treacle bread. We would be so stuffed with goodies that we had no problem going to sleep early before Santa arrived."

– Mary Curley, Lucan Guild, Dublin

Without Thy sunshine and Thy rain
We could not have the golden grain;
Without Thy love we'd not be fed;
We thank Thee for our daily bread.
Praise God, from whom all goodness flows.

– Traditional mealtime prayer

"*When I was young, Christmas started at five p.m. on Christmas Eve. All our farm jobs and housework had to be finished by then so that Christmas could begin. We all showered and dressed up in our Christmas clothes and sat down to our Christmas Eve dinner at six. We had bacon, which was boiled and roasted, served with vegetables and potatoes, including special roasted ones.*

Dessert was my mother's beautiful trifle with custard finished off with tea made from tea leaves. There was no hurry and the table was full of chatter and banter and excitement, as we had heard the man on the Radio Éireann news telling everybody that Santa Claus had left the North Pole.

To this day, five p.m. remains special in my family. When I got married I brought this tradition with me, although in later years it now takes place anytime between 21 and 24 December, depending on our children's work schedule."

– Kay Devine, Bonniconlon Guild, Mayo

SANTA'S WHEREABOUTS

"The last job my father did on Christmas Eve was to sweep the boreen in preparation for Santa. I loved that around five p.m. we would light the candle on the front window; I can still picture my father cutting a turnip in half and cutting a hole out of the centre to place the candle in it. When we had tidied the house and sat down by the fire we waited for the magic to happen. We would listen to the 'letters to Santa' being read out on the radio and I loved that beautiful voice of Noel Purcell.

And we could not wait for Santa to leave the North Pole and how lucky and special we felt when we were one of the first houses in the world that he visited. You see, our mother had died at a young age, leaving my father responsible for rearing us five young girls. So to make up for such unfortunate circumstances, Santa always visited out house first and would arrive as soon as he was finished talking on the radio.

Coincidentally our cousin would also arrive around that time laden with Christmas goods made by our lovely Auntie Mary. She would send a cooked turkey and a delicious homemade trifle with custard and cream and dotted with red cherries. While we were 'oohing and aahing' over these treats, the dog would start barking outside and my father would go out to 'check the cows in the barn' and come in telling us he saw Santa passing over. We would rush out to the front room to see five parcels neatly wrapped in brown paper and arranged in a row on the bed. I can still smell the excitement and atmosphere of sheer delight and amazement. The innocence of it all.

After we had calmed down and admired all that Santa had brought us (he always included new gymfrocks for Christmas Day Mass), we would have a supper with our cousin. This included another treasure from Auntie Mary, the homemade butter cream sponge which we had been waiting for all day long. Then we would listen as my father told stories of his Christmases long ago in the 1920s. Eventually our cousin would get on his bike to cycle home and we would go to bed as we had to be up early in the morning to attend eight o'clock Mass. I can still hear the silence in the street in the local village as the only noise was the footsteps of the people heading to the church."

– Peg Prendeville, Ballyhahill/Loughill Guild, Limerick

FROM 'THE NIGHT BEFORE CHRISTMAS'

'Twas the night before Christmas, when all through the house
Not a creature was stirring, not even a mouse.
The stockings were hung by the chimney with care
In hope that St Nicholas soon would be there.

The children were nestled all snug in their beds
While visions of sugar-plums danced in their heads ...

When, what to my wandering eye did appear
But a miniature sleigh and eight tiny reindeer.

With a little old driver, so lively and quick
I knew in a moment it must be St Nick.
More rapid than eagles his coursers they came
And he whistled and shouted and called them by name.

Now, Dasher! Now, Dancer! Now, Prancer and Vixen!
On, Comet! On, Cupid! On, Donner and Blitzen!
To the top of the porch! to the top of the wall!
Now dash away! Dash away! Dash away all! ...

And then, in a twinkling, I heard on the roof
The prancing and pawing of each little hoof.
As I drew in my head, and was turning around,
Down the chimney St Nicholas came with a bound.

He was dressed all in fur, from his head to his foot,
And his clothes were all tarnished with ashes and soot,
A bundle of toys he had flung on his back
And he looked like a peddler just opening his pack.

He spoke not a word, but went straight to his work,
And filled all the stockings, then turned with a jerk,
And laying his finger aside of his nose
And giving a nod, up the chimney he rose.

He sprang to his sleigh, to his team gave a whistle,
And away they all flew like the down of a thistle
But I heard him exclaim, 'ere he drove out of sight,
'Happy Christmas to all, and to all a good-night!'

– Clement Clarke Moore

A Merry Christmas

There's no morning like it, especially when there are children in the house, peeping over the ends of beds or creeping over thresholds just like they have done for generations, in anticipation of what magic might have unfolded in the night. Much has changed, of course – few families today walk several miles together in the pre-dawn darkness to Mass on Christmas morning – yet so much has not. The roast bird and all the trimmings, including at least two types of potato. The great debate between the defenders of sprouts and steamed puddings, and the doubters. The ones who always try to sneak into the second layer of biscuits before the first is finished. And the post-feast lull that comes as Christmas night falls and all are fed and warm.

And traditions are there for the making too. Today the Christmas morning swim draws crowds to the icy waters at the Forty Foot in Dublin or Youghal Quay in Cork. Even settling in for the Christmas Day movies that everyone's seen a thousand times has its own ritualistic appeal.

"I would wake on Christmas morning at about six o'clock. I would feel my way in the dark down the quilt until I found it. It was always there. A Christmas stocking, made of white netting and filled with little toys and trinkets. You know the ones: a Sherbet Dab; a Lucky Bag; maybe a little bugle or mouth organ; a tiny toy, perhaps a little rubber ball or a yo-yo; and always a cardboard game. Things I could fish out and play with, tucked in my bed up nice and warm in the cold bedroom until it became light enough to look on the floor at the foot of the bed and discover my 'big' present.

After breakfast, Dad would take us children out for a drive to the nearest beach, where we could run about and generally let off steam, and also to give Mum and Nellie space and time to prepare the feast. How he must have planned and scrimped on his meagre petrol ration during the 1940s 'Emergency' to be able to give us that treat! We returned home to be ushered into the dining room, which had a fire going – another luxury at a time of severe shortages of practically everything, with rationing of fuel, food, clothing, petrol."

– Imelda Byrne, Leighlinbridge Guild, Carlow

NO MORNING TO LIE IN

"It was easy to get out of bed Christmas morning. There was no lingering or hiding under the warm blankets that helped keep out the freezing winter cold. Running over the cold flagstones in the hallway, almost tripping over each other, we burst into the kitchen where on Christmas Eve we had neatly hung up over the mantelpiece the largest stockings that we could find, hoping that Santa would fill them to the brim with priceless treasures. We never noticed the cold, that our teeth chattered and goosepimples covered our feet and legs, as we eagerly examined the contents of our stockings.

Peeping over the rim were the rag dolls that Mrs Claus had so painstakingly sewn at night while we were tucked up in bed fast asleep, their hair made from strands of coloured wool plaited down the middle. We dug deeper and out came the set of blocks that we used to make Georgian houses, or the little china tea set sitting snugly in its presentation box. My sister got a wind-up cowboy with two guns strapped in a holster. We christened him Jack Ruby, this being the year President John F. Kennedy was shot dead in Dallas, Texas. There would be colouring books and the annual box of paints which, Santa knew, would keep us well occupied into the New Year. If we were lucky we might also get a fairytale book to share. Last, stuffed into the toes of the stockings, were the lovely children's hankies with the nursery rhyme print.

Once the stockings were inspected it was time to prepare for the next big event of the day. Christmas morning Mass commenced at seven a.m. and it was with great reluctance that we left our toys aside, got dressed and prepared ourselves for the mile-long journey to Tydavnet chapel. Outside it was dark and frosty and the crunch of our feet was like music on the icy road. We soon met up with our neighbours along the way and together we chatted and discussed what the great St Nicholas had brought. I wondered how my friend always got big bars of chocolate from Santa. It looked like Santa ran out of such delicacies before he reached our house!

As we neared the chapel the Christmas bell rang out in welcome. The chatter ceased and we took our places in the centre aisle sitting closely together and waited for the three Latin Masses to begin. Sometimes we slept through them, waking only when the consecration bells rang out or when our mother gave us a sharp nudge. When we came out it was daylight and soon we were on our way home, filled with anticipation for the festivities that were about to unfold."

– Patricia Cavanagh, Ballinode Guild, Monaghan

FROM 'A CHRISTMAS CHILDHOOD'

The light between the ricks of hay and straw
Was a hole in Heaven's gable. ...

Outside in the cow-house my mother
Made the music of milking;
The light of her stable-lamp was a star
And the frost of Bethlehem made it twinkle.

A water-hen screeched in the bog,
Mass-going feet
Crunched the wafer-ice on the pot-holes,
Somebody wistfully twisted the bellows wheel. ...

And I was six Christmases of age. ...

– Patrick Kavanagh

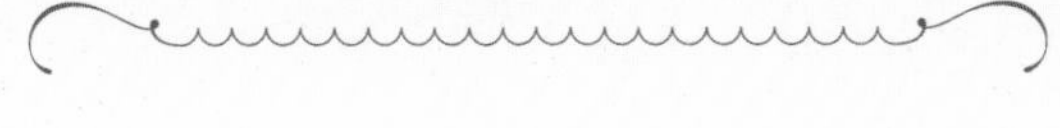

The Christmas Dinner

There's a certain logical order to cooking the Christmas meal, but it still needs co-ordination, which is one reason why it's a good idea to have prepared in advance a list of all the little jobs. That way, when someone offers to help you can delegate wisely and have the satisfaction of ticking things off the list as you go. But remember what they say about too many cooks. Sometimes a sense of calm and order is as useful as a multitude of hands. You may have done much of the prep the day before: trimming the sprouts, peeling the spuds, making the giblet stock. And if so, good for you. But if not, before you do any of that, get the bird on first, whether you're going with the aul' turkey or the old-fashioned goose (see page 195). Once that's on, you can see to all the trimmings and all the other little last-minute jobs on your list.

"On Christmas morning I heat the dinner plates in the oven and, when they are sufficiently heated, wrap them in a warm, clean towel and store them in the hot press. This frees up the oven for food later on."

– Geraldine O'Connor, Clones Guild, Monaghan

Keep starters simple – a soup from the freezer or one of the party food canapé ideas scaled up to starter size is all that is needed today. No one is going to go hungry. Remember too that if you're offering a selection of side dishes you can scale down the quantity of each.

"Christmas morning, the big fire was raging and the whole house like an oven as Mammy put the goose in the pot and laid eight or nine good big hot coals under it. The smell as our dinner cooked was delicious. The goose had been smothered in goose grease to help keep the skin tender, and some melted homemade country butter put in along with him. The stuffing was made from breadcrumbs, pepper, salt and onions. When the table was set, the goose was lifted onto the big willow pattern plate and put in the centre of the table. It was a great feast, and jelly and custard after, and plum pudding. The Christmas logs burned brightly in the fire afterwards, and the family played cards in the parlour. It was a special time, with that beautiful sleepy feeling on Christmas evening when we sat about the fire, singing songs and telling stories."

– Maura Kenny, Moore Guild, Roscommon

Roast Turkey

LIZ WALL, ASHFORD GUILD, WICKLOW

The most important thing to get right when cooking a turkey is to ensure that the bird is fully cooked. The following recipe is based on the useful instructions on www.safefood.eu, which even has a handy calculator so you can work out the best cooking time for your particular turkey.

Serves 10–12

- 5–6kg (11–13lb) turkey, giblets removed and reserved
- 15g (½oz) butter
- salt and pepper
- 500g stuffing (see page 149)

To serve

- giblet gravy (see page 148)
- roast potatoes (see page 154)
- Brussels sprouts (see pages 154 and 155)
- cranberry sauce (see page 56)
- extra vegetables or potatoes of your choice (see pages 153, 156 and 159)

ICA Tip

Take care not to overstuff your turkey. A good rule of thumb is that the ratio of stuffing to unstuffed bird should be no more than 1:10 in terms of weight.

1. Preheat oven to 180°C/350°F/Gas 4.
2. Place the bird on a roasting tray, breast side up. Rub the skin with butter and season with salt and pepper. If using a fan oven, loosely stuff the cavity of the bird with your stuffing of choice. (If using a gas oven or conventional oven, cook the stuffing separately and leave the cavity unstuffed.)
3. Cover the bird with foil. Cook in a preheated fan oven for 4 hours 20 minutes for a 5kg bird, and an extra 30 minutes for a 6kg bird. (For an unstuffed bird in a gas oven or conventional oven preheated to 180°C, reduce the cooking time by about 20 minutes.) Baste the turkey hourly to prevent it from drying out, but keep the oven door closed as much as possible to maintain the right temperature.
4. Meanwhile, make your giblet stock if you haven't done so the day before (see overleaf) and finish any prep for your vegetables and potatoes.
5. Remove the foil covering the turkey for the last 30 minutes to brown the skin. To check if the turkey is cooked, pierce the thickest part of the thigh and breast with a clean fork or skewer – the juices should run clear. If not, you may need to continue cooking for a little longer (ovens vary, so it's important to check).
6. Once fully cooked, transfer the turkey to a fresh roasting tray, re-cover with foil and set aside in a warm place to rest for at least 30 minutes before carving. This is an important step to ensure moist and juicy turkey meat.
7. Meanwhile, increase the oven heat to roast the potatoes (see pages 151 and 153) and use the roasting tray and your giblet stock to make gravy (see overleaf). If cooking the stuffing separately, moisten it with a little stock, cover with foil and bake on a lower shelf of the oven for 30 minutes.
8. Before serving, double check that the turkey is properly cooked – it should be piping hot all the way through with no pink meat left. The centre of the stuffing should also be piping hot.

Giblet Gravy

ELIZABETH MURPHY, BALLYROAN GUILD, LAOIS

Making the gravy is a two-part process, and the key to success lies in the stock. This should be made with the flavoursome parts of the bird known as the giblets, which includes the liver, heart, gizzard and neck. Ask your butcher to give you the giblets separately. You can make the stock the day before.

Serves 10–12

- goose or turkey giblets (liver, heart, gizzard, neck)
- 1 small carrot, peeled and roughly chopped
- 2–3 celery sticks, roughly chopped
- 2–3 sprigs of fresh parsley
- 1 bay leaf
- 1 tablespoon flour (or cornflour for a gluten-free gravy)

1. To make the stock for the giblet gravy, blanch and clean the heart and gizzard, wash the liver and soak the neck in cold salted water for about 30 minutes. Combine them all in a heavy-based stockpot and add about 850ml (1½ pints) of cold water.

2. Add the carrot, celery and herbs, bring to the boil and reduce to a slow simmer. Cover and simmer for 2 hours, skimming off any scum that comes to the surface. Allow to cool, then drain off the liquid, setting aside about 500ml (1 pint) to make the gravy and freezing any remaining stock for future use.

3. To make the giblet gravy, remove the bird from the roasting tin, cover in foil and set aside to rest. Pour the excess fat from the tin, keeping the brown bits stuck to the bottom of the tin. Place the tin over a moderate heat on the stovetop, and add the flour or cornflour to the roasting tin, stirring until it forms a dry brown paste.

4. Gradually stir in the heated giblet stock, stirring and reducing until it reaches the desired consistency. Stir in any juices from the resting bird, season to taste and transfer to a warmed sauce boat.

ICA *Tip*

If cooking gravy from a roast goose, you can leave a tablespoon or two of the goose fat in the roasting tray before adding the flour.

Potato Stuffing

KATHLEEN TESSYMAN, BANTRY GUILD, CORK

My Granny and my Mam would work all day on Christmas Eve getting the housework done. Then the table would be pulled out in the middle of the kitchen and they would settle down at it to make this stuffing. They peeled the boiled potatoes, and broke in a loaf of stale bread with their hands. I still make it every Christmas.

Makes about 900g

- 3 medium potatoes, or about 450g (½lb)
- 1 stale loaf of white bread, or 450g (½lb) breadcrumbs
- 2 onions, finely chopped
- 50g (2oz) butter
- 2 tablespoons mixed herbs
- 1 teaspoon mixed spice
- salt and pepper

1. Boil the potatoes in their skins in plenty of salted water. Allow to cool before peeling and breaking into a large mixing bowl. Mash the potato coarsely with a fork.

2. Blitz the stale bread into breadcrumbs, add to the potatoes and mix together.

3. Sauté the onions in the butter until soft, add the mixed herbs and mixed spice, and season to taste with salt and pepper. Add to the potato mixture, mix well and check the seasoning.

4. If you are cooking the stuffing separately or want to cook extra stuffing not used in the cavity, moisten it with a little stock, cover with foil and bake on a lower shelf of the oven, while the turkey is resting, for 30 minutes.

ICA Tip

You can add various ingredients to this basic recipe, including dried fruits such as sultanas, cranberries and apricots, or sausage meat.

May the sound of happy music
and the lilt of Irish laughter
fill your heart with gladness
that stays for ever after.

– Irish blessing

Eternal God, this joyful day is radiant with the brilliance of your one true light.
May that light illuminate our hearts and shine in our words and deeds.
May the hope, the peace, the joy and the love presented by the birth in Bethlehem
Fill our hearts and become part of all that we say and do.
May we share the divine life of your son Jesus Christ,
Even as he humbled himself to share our humanity.
Bless us and the feast you have provided for us,
Let us be thankful for the true gift of Christmas, Your Son.

Amen

– Christmas dinner blessing

May you be blessed with the spirit of the season
which is peace,
the gladness of the season
which is hope,
and the heart of the season
which is love.

– Irish Christmas blessing

Roast Potatoes

LIZ WALL, ASHFORD GUILD, WICKLOW

The perfect roast spud is a thing of beauty, and something close to many an Irish heart. Using goose fat is the first step towards perfection, but there are a few other tricks worth having up your sleeve too. Remember, if you're also serving mashed potatoes, as many Irish families like to, the quantity here should be more than enough to go with your medium-sized turkey, but you can adjust accordingly.

Serves 6–8

- 1kg (2.2lb) potatoes, peeled and cut into evenly sized pieces
- 2 teaspoons flour
- 110g (4oz) goose or duck fat

ICA Tip

The trick to getting a really crisp potato is to ensure the fat is very hot before you add the potatoes, and to use a large enough tin so that the potatoes are in a single layer.

1. Heat a roasting tin in an oven preheated to 180°C/350°F/ Gas 4.

2. Place the prepared potatoes in a large pan and pour in enough water to barely cover them. Bring to the boil and immediately reduce the heat. Simmer, uncovered, for 2 minutes.

3. Drain the potatoes in a colander. Shake back and forth a few times to fluff them up. Sprinkle with flour and give another shake so that they are evenly coated.

4. Melt the goose fat in the preheated roasting tin and heat it on the stovetop until very hot. Carefully transfer the potatoes into the fat. Take care, as they will sizzle. Roll them around so that they are well coated and spread them out in a single layer.

5. Roast for about 40 minutes or until golden and crisp, turning them twice to ensure that they are all evenly coloured.

Hasselback Potatoes

MAURA RIORDAN, DUN LAOGHAIRE GUILD, DUBLIN

This is an unusual way to cook potatoes that originate in Sweden. Each potato half is sliced almost to the base and then roasted skin-on with oil and butter.

Serves 6–8

- 12–15 medium potatoes, scrubbed but not peeled
- 4 tablespoons olive oil or goose fat
- 50g (2oz) butter
- sea salt

You'll also need

- roasting tray
- pastry brush

1. Preheat oven to 190°C/375°F/Gas 5.
2. Cut each potato in half lengthways. Place each half flat-side down on the chopping board and use a sharp chef's knife to cut down as if making very thin slices, but leaving the bottom 1cm (½in) intact.
3. Heat a large roasting tray on the stovetop and melt the butter and oil until sizzling. Transfer the prepared potatoes, flat side down, to the roasting tray, and brush the tops generously with the hot butter and oil.
4. Season with sea salt flakes and bake in the preheated oven until they begin to brown, about 40–50 minutes depending on the size of the potatoes.

Saucy Brussels Sprouts

MARION LYON, MAGHERA GUILD, CAVAN

I picked up this recipe back in the late 1970s and have been using it since. As with all Brussels sprouts recipes, the trick to is not to overcook them. This sauce makes them extra delicious.

Serves 6–8

- 450g (1lb) Brussels sprouts
- 1 small onion, chopped
- 25g (1oz) butter
- 1 tablespoon plain flour
- 1 tablespoon brown sugar
- 1 teaspoon salt
- ½ teaspoon dry mustard
- 150ml (¼ pint) milk
- 275ml (½ pint) sour cream

1. To prepare the Brussels sprouts, remove any larger outer leaves, trim the bases and cut a shallow cross into the base of each sprout. Cook, covered, in a small amount of boiling salted water until tender but still crisp, about 10–15 minutes. Drain well.

2. Meanwhile, in a medium saucepan, gently sweat the onion in butter until soft but not brown.

3. Stir in the flour, sugar, salt and mustard and then the milk. Cook, stirring constantly, until thickened.

4. Stir in the sour cream. Add the cooked Brussels sprouts and stir gently to combine. Continue to cook until heated through, but do not allow to boil.

Stir-fried Brussels Sprouts

MAURA RIORDAN, DUN LAOGHAIRE GUILD, DUBLIN

The addition of a little ginger heat to the sprouts in this recipe gives an interesting dimension, while stir-frying is a great way to ensure that these oft-abused vegetables are not over-cooked.

Serves 6–8

- 450g (1lb) Brussels sprouts
- 1 tablespoon sunflower oil
- 6–8 scallions, cut into 2.5cm (1in) lengths
- 2 slices peeled fresh root ginger
- 4 tablespoons sliced almonds (optional)
- 4 tablespoons vegetable stock

1. To prepare the Brussels sprouts, remove any larger outer leaves and trim the bases. Cut lengthways into 1cm (½in) slices.

2. Heat the oil in a wok or heavy-based frying pan, and fry the scallions and ginger for two or three minutes, stirring frequently. Add the almonds, if using, and continue to stir-fry over a moderate heat until the onions and almonds begin to brown.

3. Remove and discard the ginger, reduce the heat and stir in the sliced Brussels sprouts. Stir-fry for a few minutes before adding the vegetable stock. Cook over a gentle heat for a further 5–6 minutes or until the sprouts are almost tender. Transfer to a heated serving dish and keep warm until ready to serve.

ICA Tip

Take care not to overcook the sprouts as they will continue to cook in their own heat, and you'll want to keep them warm for a few minutes while you finish off any last-minute jobs before serving the big meal.

Whipped Parsnips and Sweet Potatoes

MARION LYON, MAGHERA GUILD, CAVAN

Parsnips can be roasted to bring out their sweetness, but if you'd prefer a stove-top recipe, the addition of sweet potatoes is another way of bringing out the sweetness of the parsnips.

Serves 6–8

- 450g (1lb) parsnips
- 450g (1lb) sweet potatoes
- 2 tablespoons butter
- ½ teaspoon salt
- ¼ teaspoon ground allspice

To finish

- milk (optional)
- finely sliced scallions (optional)
- extra butter

1. Peel and slice the parsnips and sweet potatoes.
2. In a covered pan, cook the vegetables in a little boiling salted water until tender, about 15 minutes.
3. Drain and transfer to a large mixing bowl. Add butter, salt and allspice, and beat until smooth and fluffy. You may wish to add a little milk to loosen. Top with sliced scallions, if using, and more butter for extra flavour. Check seasoning before serving.

Pennsylvania Red Cabbage

MARION LYON, MAGHERA GUILD, CAVAN

A family favourite, this red cabbage dish is Pennsylvania Dutch. My husband is from Pennsylvania and I probably got this recipe from his mother, Clovena, or his Aunt Elda, although I've been making it so long I no longer remember! It's in cups but if you don't have measuring cups, just use a regular teacup; it's the ratio rather than the quantity that is important.

Serves 4–6

- 2 tablespoons bacon dripping
- ¼ cup packed brown sugar
- ¼ cup vinegar
- ¼ cup water
- 1½ teaspoon salt
- dash pepper
- ½ teaspoon caraway seeds
- 4 cups shredded red cabbage
- 2 cups cubed, unpeeled apple

1. Heat the bacon dripping in a large heavy-based frying pan. Stir in the brown sugar, vinegar, water, salt, pepper and caraway seeds.

2. Add the red cabbage and apple, stirring to coat well. Cover and cook over a low heat, stirring occasionally. If you prefer a crisp cabbage, cook for 15 minutes; for well-cooked cabbage, cook for 25–30 minutes.

“Our Christmas dinner was the traditional turkey and ham with celery in white sauce, Brussels sprouts, roast potatoes and mashed, not forgetting bread sauce and carrots and marrowfat peas soaked the night before with bread soda. Dessert always included plum pudding, brought to the table, where my mother poured warmed brandy over it and lit it. But the highlight of the desserts was always the sherry trifle.

My mother would line the special cut-glass bowl we used for the occasion with store-bought madeira or sponge cake and soak it with about three tablespoons of sherry. Then she would add a tin of well-drained fruit salad (although of course today you can use fresh fruit like strawberries), pour over a layer of thick custard and finally another layer of well-beaten cream to top it. There were never any trifle leftovers – unlike the turkey, which we ate for days!”

– Anne Payne, Portlaoise Guild, Laois

“My mother would cook a turkey that she had reared for the festive season. Our immediate neighbour, a widower and senior citizen, always refused the invitation to join us on Christmas day. In our parish no one crossed another family's threshold on that holy day. Instead my brother and I were dispatched with his turkey dinner, with strict instructions to hand it to him across the half door! Needless to say we weren't invited in then, or when we returned with the plum pudding. My mother's plum pudding was the most delicious that I have ever tasted. I have always used her recipe but it never seemed to taste as good as hers.”

– Connie McEvoy, Termonfeckin Guild, Louth

Brown Sugar Sauce for Plum Pudding

STEPHANIE IGOE, ENNYBEGS GUILD, LONGFORD

My Grandma's recipe for a simple sauce to accompany the Christmas pudding has become a family favourite, and has been passed on to aunts and uncles, cousins, grandchildren and even great grandchildren.

Serves 8 (to accompany a medium-sized pudding)

- 110g (4oz) butter
- 110g (4oz) flour
- 600g (1lb 5oz) brown sugar
- 1.2 litres (2 pints) boiling water
- 2 teaspoons vanilla extract

1. In a medium-sized saucepan over a medium heat, melt the butter and add the flour, stirring constantly.

2. Add the brown sugar and continue to stir until the sugar gains a deeper brown colour.

3. Add boiling water (be careful with this step as the water will really sizzle when it is added) and stir until smooth. Boil the sauce for two or three minutes before removing from the heat and stirring in the vanilla.

Whiskey Sauce for Plum Pudding

ROSEMARY MCCARVILLE, CLONES GUILD, MONAGHAN

Christmas wouldn't be Christmas without plum pudding, or so the saying goes. This is a sauce to make it really special. It uses cornflour, so it's a gluten-free alternative to a traditional flour-based white sauce. The use of whiskey instead of brandy gives it a particularly Irish flavour.

Makes 275ml (½ pint)

- 1 tablespoon cornflour
- 1 tablespoon sugar
- 275ml (½ pint) milk
- 15g (½oz) butter
- 2 tablespoons whiskey (or brandy)

1. Blend the cornflour, sugar and a little of the milk in a bowl to form a smooth paste.

2. Bring the remaining milk to the boil in a small saucepan. Pour this gradually over the cornflour mixture, mixing as you do to blend, and then transfer the lot back into the saucepan and return to the heat.

3. Bring back to the boil, stirring all the time. Reduce to a simmer and cook gently until thickened.

4. Stir in the butter and whiskey. Transfer to a preheated jug. If not using immediately, cover the surface of the sauce with cling film and set aside somewhere warm until required.

Brandy Sauce for Plum Pudding

LIZ WALL, ASHFORD GUILD, WICKLOW

This is a traditional white sauce flavoured with brandy and served hot with steamed plum pudding. It is essentially a sweetened, boozy version of a classic béchamel sauce, which is a very useful sauce to master.

Makes about 300ml (10fl oz)

- 50g (2oz) butter
- 50g (2oz) plain flour
- 300ml (10fl oz) full fat milk
- 50g (2oz) golden caster sugar
- 2 tablespoons brandy
- 125ml (4fl oz) double cream

1. Gently melt the butter in a medium-sized saucepan over a medium heat, add the flour and stir well to make a paste. Add in the milk little by little, whisking vigorously as you do, until the mixture reaches simmering point and begins to thicken.

2. Reduce the heat to its lowest setting, stir in the sugar and cook gently for a further 10 minutes.

3. Stir in the brandy and cream, cook for another minute to heat through and transfer to a preheated jug. Cover the surface of the sauce with clingfilm and set aside somewhere warm until required.

A Time to Unwind

St Stephen's Day is another special day in Ireland. Traditionally in many areas it was synonymous with Wren's Day, which took various forms but generally involved dressing up and parading about the neighbourhood singing traditional songs. For other families, St Stephen's Day has been a sacred day of rest after all the hard work leading up to the main festivities. A lazy day for lie-ins and breakfasts in bed.

"*Mum and Dad were clever with our presents. They always included annuals like* the Beano, *the* Dandy, Bunty *and* Judy, *which ensured for them a good lie-in on* St Stephen's Day. *We were allowed to go down in our dressing gowns to raid the kitchen and bring our breakfast back up to bed. Stephen's Day breakfast usually consisted of goose and stuffing sandwiches, Christmas cake and red lemonade for all of us except for my brother. He always cut a huge wedge of plum pudding, fried it in about a week's rations of butter, smothered it in golden syrup and took a siphon of lemonade back up to his bed!*"

– Imelda Byrne, Leighlinbridge Guild, Carlow

It was a day to regroup, to sit and chat or read that new book, to take a brisk walk if the weather permitted or play cards with neighbours if it didn't. For some it was a day of abstinence to rebalance the previous day's indulgence.

"*The strictly adhered-to custom in my parents' south Leitrim household was to abstain from meat and fish on St Stephen's Day. The fare on the day usually consisted of porridge for breakfast, vegetable soup for midday dinner and a boiled egg for supper. My late father told me that the practice was observed in rural households in the belief that it would ward off contagious diseases for the following year. The custom seems to be rare or has all but died out. Few, if any, of my friends or neighbours have heard of the tradition of abstinence on the 26th. But when I married and settled in Longford, lo and behold, my husband's family had the same tradition. I think it is a lovely custom and we have continued to observe it.*"

– Helen O'Shea, Newtowncashel Guild, Longford

For others it remains a day when light grazing of delicious leftovers is in order. Certainly, picking any remaining meat off the leftover turkey and making a stock with the carcass is a sensible thing to do, especially if you're not going to eat it that day but want to set it aside for the coming days. Part of the pleasure of the days following the Christmas feast is coming up with novel ways to repurpose the leftovers into delicious new treats.

Turkey Chowder

IRENE O'BRIEN, SCOTSHOUSE GUILD, MONAGHAN

A leftover turkey offers the opportunity both to use the carcass for a stock and to use the pickings of meat too. This recipe utilises both, and is a nice way to use the bitty little pieces of turkey meat that you mightn't put in a sandwich or platter of cold cuts, including the dark meat which of course offers the most flavour.

Serves 6–8

- 675g (1½lb) potatoes, peeled and chopped
- 1 onion, chopped
- 1 leek, sliced
- 2 cloves garlic, sliced
- vegetable or rapeseed oil, for frying
- 1½ litres (2½ pints) turkey or chicken stock
- 2 bacon rashers, diced
- 2 handfuls fresh sage leaves, finely chopped
- 250g (9oz) cooked turkey, torn or roughly chopped
- 1 bunch scallions, chopped
- 150ml (¼ pint) double cream

For the stock

- turkey carcass, picked clean of leftover meat
- 2–3 sticks of celery, roughly chopped
- 1–2 carrots, peeled and roughly chopped
- 1 onion, halved
- 1 teaspoon peppercorns
- 1 bay leaf

To garnish

- 2–3 handfuls fresh parsley, chopped

1. To make the stock, pick the carcass clean of all leftover meat and place in a large heavy-based stockpot along with the celery, carrots, onion, peppercorns and bay leaf. Top up with water, bring to the boil and reduce to a simmer for an hour or two, periodically skimming off any scum that rises to the surface. Strain off the liquid and discard the bones and seasonings.

2. In a large heavy-based pot, sweat the potatoes, onion, leek and garlic in a little oil for a few minutes, then top up with the stock and simmer gently until the potatoes are tender.

3. In a separate pan, fry the diced bacon with the chopped sage. Add to the soup along with the turkey meat, scallions and cream.

4. Serve in warm bowls sprinkled with chopped parsley.

ICA Tip

You can add other aromatics to your stock if you have them, such as a sprig of fresh thyme or the trimmings of a fennel bulb. It's handy to keep these in a ziplock bag in the freezer for popping into a stock anytime you're making one.

Bacon, Cheese and Pear Toasties

ANNE MARIA DENNISON, MAINISTIR NA FÉILE GUILD, LIMERICK

A great way to use up leftover cheese for a light lunch, the toasties can also be cut into bite-sized slices and served with salad leaves as a tasty starter, or with a hearty turkey chowder or ribollita soup (page 19) defrosted from the freezer. If served as a starter, it can be prepared and assembled in advance and simply finished off under the grill before serving.

Serves 2

- 4 rashers smoked bacon
- 2 thick slices of bread, white or brown
- 140g (5oz) leftover Brie or blue cheese
- 1 large ripe pear, cored

To serve

- 2 handfuls salad leaves
- 2 cherry tomatoes, sliced
- redcurrant or apple jelly

1. Grill the rashers until cooked but not crisp. Chop into bite-sized pieces and set aside.

2. Lightly toast the bread on one side under a hot grill. Meanwhile, thinly slice the pear and cheese.

3. To assemble, put a layer of sliced pear on the un-toasted side of bread, then scatter over a layer of chopped bacon. Top with slices of the cheese. (You can set it aside at this point until ready to serve.)

4. Before serving, place under a hot grill for a few minutes or until the cheese begins to melt. Serve immediately with some salad leaves, sliced cherry tomatoes and redcurrant or apple jelly, if using.

ICA *Tip*

If you don't have a ripe pear, use a drained tin of pears instead.

Curried Turkey Salad

MARION LYON, MAGHERA GUILD, CAVAN

This curried salad is best served well chilled, so it can be made up in advance for grazing on when appetite demands. The crunch of the apple and the tang of the yoghurt give it a welcome freshness after all the rich food of Christmas Day itself.

Serves 4–6

- 600g (1lb 5oz) cooked turkey meat
- 2 apples, red or green
- ¼ lemon, juice only
- 125ml (4fl oz) good-quality mayonnaise
- 125ml (4fl oz) natural yoghurt
- 1 shallot or small onion, finely diced
- 2 tablespoons curry powder
- salt and freshly ground pepper
- 3–4 scallions, chopped
- 3–4 handfuls picked parsley leaves, finely chopped

To serve

- mixed green leaves such as watercress or rocket
- simple oil and lemon dressing
- crusty bread

1. Dice the turkey meat and place in a large mixing bowl. Quarter, core and finely dice the apples and toss in a little water acidulated with a squeeze of lemon juice to prevent oxidation.

2. In a separate bowl, blend together the mayonnaise, yoghurt, onion and curry powder, and season to taste with salt, pepper and about two tablespoons of lemon juice.

3. Add the dressing to the turkey and toss well to blend. Add the scallions and parsley and toss lightly. Cover and chill until ready to serve.

4. Serve with a crisp salad of green leaves such as watercress or rocket tossed lightly in a simple oil and lemon juice dressing, and with slices of crusty bread on the side.

ICA Tip

We eat with our eyes, and adding a little extra colour can do wonders for a sluggish appetite. Consider slicing a generous handful of red grapes and scattering over the salad before serving.

HUNTING THE WREN

"St Stephen's Day might be considered a quiet day for some, but not in Dingle, County Kerry, where it is known as the Wren's Day (pronounced 'wran'). This day has a special significance in the life and culture of the area. Groups of musicians, figures dressed in straw suits and followers in fancy dress or disguise can be seen about the streets of the town, 'hunting the wren'. This very ancient tradition still survives strongly in Dingle.

There are a number of wren groups around the town: the Green and Gold Wren, John Street Wren, the Quay Wren and Goat Street Wren. From early in the morning and throughout the day they parade around the town, dressed in colourful costumes and disguises, led by the powerful sounds of the fife and drum bands. They go door to door and pub to pub collecting money for various charities. Each group also visits the local community hospital where they provide plenty of entertainment and fun. On their way they tease and pick on those bystanders they know."

– Dora Kennedy, Annascaul Guild, Kerry

"Although Wren's Day on 26 December is typically associated with men dressed up in straw costumes 'hunting the wren', in our local area the day was less dramatic. Disguises like face colouring, pieces of netting over people's faces or towels on their heads were more common. I remember it as an exciting day connected with song and music.

Walking was our mode of transport – or a bicycle, with strict orders to 'keep well in' to the side of the road. As small children we were allowed to go with an older sister or neighbour to the near neighbours' houses, where we sang or Christmas carols such as 'Away in a Manger'.

Hours were spent dressing up to disguise ourselves with pieces of net curtain draped over our faces and held in place with an old hat or cap. Boys' trousers and wellingtons completed the simple costume. We shyly shuffled in to the kitchens of kind neighbours who listened and complimented us and then we shook our empty cocoa tin with a slit in the lid. Low-value coins (a shilling, sixpence or even threepence) were dropped in and then they tried to guess who was under the disguise. When we were tired we trudged home with our share of the money collected and looked forward to the evening when groups of adult 'wren boys' came to visit the house."

– Ada Vance, Killeshandra Guild, Cavan

Wren's Day Bubble and Squeak

JANET MURPHY, CLOCHAN/BHREANAINN GUILD, KERRY

Bubble and squeak is an essential part of traditional Wren's Day eating for my husband and four sons. It is a simple and extremely useful method of using up leftovers from Christmas dinner. The recipe came with me when I 'blew in' from England to West Kerry back in 1979.

- leftover Brussels sprouts
- leftover mashed potato
- salt and pepper
- butter

To serve
- cold turkey or ham
- salad or vegetables

1. Mash the leftover Brussels sprouts into the leftover mashed potato, and season with salt and pepper. Form into round cakes.

2. Melt a knob of butter in a heavy-based frying pan, and when it's hot, add the cake of mashed potato and sprouts. Fry slowly until the base is golden brown, then turn and gently fry the other side until heated through.

3. Serve as a simple supper with cold cuts of turkey or ham, a simple salad or reheated vegetables if you prefer.

THE CHRISTMAS BRACK

"One of the vivid memories I have of my childhood Christmas is of the 'Christmas box' received from those grocers' shops used most regularly by our family. This would often include a large fruit brack among other treats. Other shops that were used from time to time also gave some small gift as a token of their appreciation, and this was almost always a Christmas brack. On one Christmas I remember there being as many as three or four bracks in the house.

Of course, with all the other goodies like Mother's rich Christmas cake and coffee sponge as well as chocolate biscuits, the bracks were often forgotten in the bottom of the bread bin for some days. Never one to waste, our multi-talented mother found ways to make them attractive. One was her version of bread and butter pudding, but made with fruit brack. Another simple way was to cut into slices about an inch wide and fry in the homemade butter that was made every week in the small dairy attached to our farmhouse kitchen.

I remember one mid-morning when the menfolk had been fed and had gone off happy, leaving Mother and myself with the tidying up. Out came the big black cast iron frying pan, and we had our mug of tea and two slices of the lovely rich brack fried in sizzling butter with a dollop of cream. We're talking real cream, which was skimmed from the top of the enamel bucket of milk brought in twice daily after the milking. I remember Mother saying, 'This is as good as Christmas pudding.' It certainly was, if millions of calories!"

– Ada Vance, Killeshandra Guild, Cavan

Brack and Butter Pudding

ADA VANCE, KILLESHANDRA GUILD, CAVAN

This is my version of what Mammy baked all those years ago – I've made it from memory over the years as she measured by handfuls rather than working to a written recipe. The marmalade is my addition; it makes the bread fantastically crisp, and gives a zingy tang.

Serves 6

- 1 good-quality fruit brack
- 85g (3oz) unsalted butter, room temperature
- good pinch of ground nutmeg
- good pinch of ground cinnamon
- 4 large eggs, preferably free-range or organic
- 400ml (¾ pint) whole milk
- 150ml (¼ pint) double cream
- 100g (3½ oz) caster sugar
- 1 teaspoon vanilla extract
- 3–4 tablespoons good-quality marmalade

To serve

- cream or ice cream

You'll also need

- large ovenproof dish or roasting tin
- pastry brush

1. Cut the brack into eight 2cm (1in) slices. Use a little of the butter to grease an ovenproof dish or roasting tin. Preheat oven to 200°C/400°F/Gas 6.

2. Blend together the remaining butter and the ground nutmeg and cinnamon. Spread evenly over the slices of brack and then cut the slices diagonally. Layer the brack neatly and evenly in the dish or tin.

3. Beat together the eggs, milk, cream and sugar, add the vanilla and pour evenly over the dish, completely covering the brack. Allow to sit for 10–15 minutes so that the brack absorbs the liquid, then brush the marmalade over the top.

4. Bake in the preheated oven for 10 minutes, then reduce the heat to 180°C/350°F/Gas 4 and continue cooking for a further 30–40 minutes or until the pudding is puffed up and crisp on top. The inside should be nicely set but still moist and a little wobbly. Remember that the egg will continue cooking and you don't want to let it dry out.

5. Serve warm with cream or ice cream.

ICA Tip

If you don't have a grocer giving you brack, you could make this with leftover Christmas bread or make the Báirín Breac recipe from *The ICA Book of Home and Family*, page 95.

Mincemeat Muddle

IRENE O'BRIEN, SCOTSHOUSE GUILD, MONAGHAN

This is an easy and attractive way to rustle up a festive dessert with little notice, using some leftover mincemeat along with a few other useful standby ingredients: some shop-bought meringues, a few squares of quality chocolate and a little whipped cream.

Serves 4–6

- 4–6 tablespoons mincemeat
- 4 tablespoons brandy
- 240ml (9fl oz) double cream
- 4 meringues (shop-bought are handy)

To garnish

- good-quality chocolate of choice, grated

1. Gently warm the mincemeat through and stir in the brandy. Set aside to cool.
2. Whip the cream until it forms soft peaks and crumble in the meringues.
3. Once the mincemeat has cooled, place it in the base of a serving dish and cover with cream and meringue. Chill for 20 minutes or until ready to serve.
4. Before serving, sprinkle with grated chocolate.

ICA Tip

You could flavour the cream with a little orange or clementine zest for an extra festive effect.

Christmas Pudding Ice Cream

CATHERINE GALLAGHER, NEWTOWNCASHEL GUILD, LONGFORD

I got this recipe from my late aunt, Kathleen McGoey, many years ago. I use it almost every Christmas as there is always some Christmas pudding left over. It's a nice way to stretch those Christmas flavours out over the festive season and, if well wrapped, it'll keep well for several weeks in the freezer.

Makes 900g (2lb) loaf-size block

- 400ml (¾ pint) double cream
- 450g (1lb) custard (ready-made will do)
- 1 tablespoon brandy
- 110g (4oz) leftover Christmas pudding
- 50g (2oz) sultanas
- 110g (4oz) red and green glacé cherries, chopped

You'll also need

- 900g (2lb) loaf tin or equivalent-sized freezer-safe container

1. In a large mixing bowl, whisk the cream until thick. Gently fold in the custard and brandy.

2. Crumble the Christmas pudding into a separate bowl and mix with the sultanas and half the chopped cherries. Carefully fold this mixture into the custard and cream.

3. Spoon into a loaf tin or plastic food container and level the top. Cover and place in the fast freeze compartment of the freezer for at least 4 hours or until solid.

4. Dip the loaf tin into a bowl of hot water for a few seconds then turn onto a serving plate. Arrange the remaining half of the cherries on top of the ice cream and serve immediately.

ICA Tip

Other nice ways to use up leftover Christmas pudding are to fry it in butter and serve with brandy cream (sinful, but delicious – especially after a cold winter's walk) or to crumble into melted chocolate to make little Christmas truffles.

Julia Carty (RIP) was a lifetime member of the ICA. She passed away in February 2015 at the age of 91. The following extract is taken word for word from a little essay the young Julia (née Gaffey) wrote in National School about local festival customs.

Every year we celebrate a great feast in honour of St Stephen. It is held on the twentysixth of December. The night before, the little boys go too a neighbouring house that is thatched, and search for a wren.

When the find a wren they bring it home, and put it in a cage. The next morning the get up very early and eat a good breakfast. The rime they sing is 'the wren the wren the King of all birds, St Stephen's day she was caught in the furze, all though he was little his family was great, rise up landlady and give him a treat. All silver and no brass half a crown is not much, but it is up with the kettle and down with the pan to comfort yourself and your jolly old man.'

– Julia Carty (RIP), Moore Guild, Roscommon

The Wren, the Wren, the king of all birds
St Stephen's Day he was caught in the furze
Although he is little, his honour is great,
Rise up, kind sir, and give us a trate.

We followed this Wren ten miles or more,
Through hedges and ditches and heaps of snow.
We up with our wattles and gave him a fall,
And brought him here to show to all.

For we are the boys that come your way,
To bury the Wren on St Stephen's Day
So up with the kettle and down with the pan,
And give us some help to bury the Wren.

– Traditional

White Chocolate and Cranberry Blondies

LIZ WALL, ASHFORD GUILD, WICKLOW

This seasonal take on traditional chocolate brownies is a lovely treat to enjoy in the quieter days post-Christmas, whether curled up with a book or mid-hike on top of a mountain. They are also versatile enough to cut into small squares and serve as an elegant bite with post-dinner coffee.

Makes 12 large slices or 24–30 small squares

- 200g (7oz) butter
- 300g (10oz) good-quality white chocolate, chopped
- 3 medium eggs
- 150g (5½oz) caster sugar
- ½ teaspoon vanilla extract
- 200g (7oz) self-raising flour, sieved
- pinch of salt
- 110g (4oz) dried cranberries
- 1–2 handfuls flaked almonds (optional)

To serve

- icing sugar

You'll also need

- 20cm x 30cm (8in x 12in) baking tin
- baking parchment

1. Preheat oven to 180°C/350°F/Gas 4. Lightly grease a baking tin and line the base with baking parchment.

2. Gently melt the butter and half the chocolate in a bain marie (a heatproof bowl set over a gently simmering saucepan of water), whisking together until smooth. Set aside to cool a little.

3. In a separate bowl, beat together the eggs, sugar and vanilla until pale, then add the melted white chocolate mixture and beat to integrate.

4. Fold in the sieved flour and salt, and then the remaining chocolate and most of the cranberries, reserving a few. Add the flaked almonds, if using, and mix well.

5. Pour into the prepared baking tin, scatter over the reserved cranberries, and bake in a preheated oven for 25 minutes or until the top is firm and lightly golden.

6. Remove and allow to cool in the pan before cutting into squares or rectangles of the required size. Store in an airtight container where they will keep for three to four days, or up to a week in the fridge. They also freeze well.

7. Dust lightly with icing sugar before serving.

ICA Tip

The flaked almonds lend some extra texture to the fruit, but you could replace the cranberries altogether and use chocolate chips instead, with or without chopped nuts.

Baked Alaska

BETTY GORMAN, CASTLETOWN GUILD, LAOIS

The combination of thick meringue straight out of a hot oven and cold ice cream in the centre never fails to impress and yet, as much of the preparation can be done in advance, it only takes about 10 minutes to assemble and serve. It must be eaten at once, but that won't be a problem.

Serves 6

For the base

- 2 eggs
- 50g (2oz) caster sugar
- 75g (2½oz) plain flour

For the topping

- 3 egg whites
- 125g (4½oz) caster sugar
- 2 tablespoons sherry
- 1 family-size block of vanilla ice-cream (1 litre)

You'll also need

- Swiss roll tin
- baking parchment

1. Preheat oven to 180°C/350°F/Gas 4. Grease a Swiss roll tin and line with baking parchment.

2. In a heatproof bowl over a pan of simmering water, whisk the whole eggs and sugar together until the mixture is thick and creamy.

3. Remove the bowl from the pan, sieve in the flour and fold gently to incorporate. Spread this mixture evenly in the prepared tin and bake in the preheated oven for 20 minutes.

4. Allow to cool on a wire tray before gently removing the baking parchment. This sponge can be wrapped in greaseproof paper and stored in an airtight container for 3 or 4 days.

5. When ready to serve, preheat oven to 220°C/425°F/Gas 7. Meanwhile, whisk the egg whites until stiff and gently fold in the sugar.

6. To assemble, transfer the sponge base to a heatproof serving dish, drizzle over the sherry and arrange the ice cream on top, leaving a space of at least 1cm (½in) from the sides. Spread the whisked egg white mixture over the ice-cream, sealing in the sponge all around.

7. Bake in the preheated oven for 4 minutes and serve immediately.

ICA Tip

If you have a chef's blow torch, you can scorch the meringue before serving to give it a caramelised outer layer.

Pineapple Fruit Cake

ANNE MARIA DENNISON, MAINISTIR NA FÉILE GUILD, LIMERICK

Pineapples were the height of fashion in the great houses of Georgian Ireland, and a symbol of great wealth. Today a tin of pineapple is an affordable convenience for when you crave some fruit in the middle of winter. This light, moist cake is quick and easy, and makes a nice alternative to richer Christmas cakes.

Makes 2 x 900g (2lb) loaves

- 400g (14oz) tinned pineapple
- 140g (5oz) sugar
- 110g (4oz) butter or margarine
- 175g (6oz) self-raising flour
- 175g (6oz) plain flour
- 1 teaspoon bicarbonate of soda
- 1 teaspoon mixed spice
- 450g (1lb) mixed dried fruit
- 2 eggs, beaten
- a few glacé cherries (optional)

You'll also need

- 2 x 900g (2lb) loaf tins
- baking parchment

1. Drain the juice from the tin of pineapple into a small saucepan. Crush the fruit in a blender (if not already crushed) and add to the saucepan together with the sugar and butter. Bring to the boil, stir to mix well, and simmer for 3 minutes. Allow to cool.

2. Meanwhile, sieve the self-raising flour, plain flour, soda and spice together into a large mixing bowl.

3. Preheat the oven to 170°C/325°F/Gas 3. Line both loaf tins with baking parchment.

4. Once the pineapple has cooled, add it to the dried fruit and mix well. Combine the fruit with the dry ingredients and the beaten eggs and mix well.

5. Divide between the two prepared tins, and scatter over a few cherries, if using. Bake on the middle shelf of the preheated oven for 90 minutes.

6. Allow to cool before removing from the tin. Wrap in greaseproof paper and foil until ready to serve.

Rich Fruit Tart

MAURA RIORDAN, DUN LAOGHAIRE GUILD, DUBLIN

This is a seasonal favourite from my recipe scrapbook. It looks as festive as it tastes, and the addition of pears and prunes gives extra depth of flavour to the classic apple pie that has been so popular in Irish households for so many years.

Makes 23cm (9in) tart

- 300g (10½oz) plain flour
- 1 tablespoon caster sugar
- 200g (7oz) butter
- 2 egg yolks (size 1)

For the filling

- 50g (2oz) butter
- 2 large cooking apples, peeled, cored, quartered and cubed
- 2 pears, peeled, cored and chopped
- 125g (4½oz) raisins
- 125g (4½oz) pitted prunes, chopped
- 1 lemon, zest and juice

To finish

- 1 egg white, beaten
- 1 tablespoon chopped almonds
- 1 tablespoon granulated sugar

To garnish

- icing sugar

You'll also need

- 23cm (9in) loose-bottomed tart tin

1. Sieve the flour into a large mixing bowl and add the sugar. Rub the butter into the flour until it forms crumbs. Add the egg yolks and mix well to form a dough. Wrap in cling film and chill for about 30 minutes.

2. Meanwhile, to make the filling, melt the butter in a large pan over a high heat. When it is hot, add the prepped apples and pears and cook for a few minutes until soft.

3. Add the raisins, prunes and lemon zest and juice and cook until reduced to a moist but slightly sticky consistency. Set aside to cool.

4. Preheat oven to 200°C/400°F/Gas 6. Grease a tart tin.

5. Roll out the pastry and transfer to the prepared tin, pressing the pastry down into the corners and sides of the tin. Cut away the excess pastry. Fill the pastry case with the cooked apple filling.

6. Re-roll the pastry trimmings and cut out star shapes to decorate the top of the tart. Brush the stars with beaten egg white and sprinkle with chopped almonds and granulated sugar. Place the tart on a baking tray and bake in a preheated oven for 20 minutes or until golden.

7. Serve the tart warm, and dust the stars with a little icing sugar before serving.

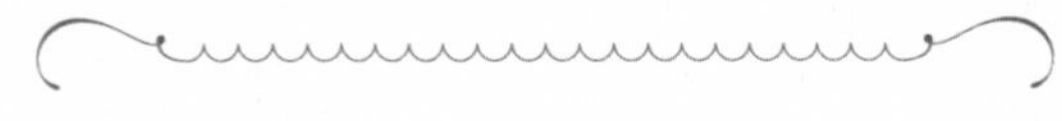

The Twelve Days of Christmas

There are those who claim that this old and beloved carol is Ireland's very own. The story is that 'The Twelve Days of Christmas' was written as a catechism song to help young Catholics learn the tenets of their faith, during a time when the practice of Catholicism was banned under the rule of the English monarch.

Each of the gifts in the song can be linked to key teachings of the faith: the eleven pipers piping representing the eleven faithful apostles; six geese a-laying for the six days of creation; the four calling birds are the Four Evangelists and their Gospels. And as for the one true love? We'll let you guess that one.

Of course, there's another quintessentially Irish version of this beloved carol, and that is the one very tongue-in-cheek recording that you'll catch on the airwaves at least once every Christmas. It's performed by none other than Father Jack himself, or his alter ego, the actor Frank Kelly. It begins well, with the partridge settling in beside the two turtle doves on the pear-tree, which stands in a bucket in the sitting room. By day five, however, things have taken a turn for the worse ...

FROM 'THE TWELVE DAYS OF CHRISTMAS'

DAY FIVE

Nuala,
Your generosity knows no bounds. Five gold rings! When the parcel arrived I was scared stiff that it might be more birds, because the smell in the living-room is atrocious. However, I don't want to seem ungrateful for the beautiful rings.
Your affectionate friend, Gobnait

DAY SIX

Nuala,
What are you trying to do to us? It isn't that we don't appreciate your generosity but the six geese have not alone nearly murdered the calling birds but they laid their eggs on top of the vet's head from the pear-tree and his bill was £68 in cash! My mother is munching 60 grains of Valium a day and talking to herself in a most alarming way. You must keep your feelings for me in check.
Gobnait

– Frank Kelly

The Last of the Feasting

Christmas Day might be come and gone for another year, and St Stephen's Day too, but that doesn't mean that the Christmas celebrations are over. Far from it. In Ireland, we know well that there are twelve days of Christmas, and the holidays continue right through into the New Year and up as far as the Feast of the Epiphany on 6 January. This is the day – and not a day sooner – that the Christmas tree comes down, and the decorations go back in their box for another year. (Don't forget to box them up into separate boxes for each room, and label them, just as we suggest on page 77.)

The twelfth night of Christmas is also known rather fondly as Little Christmas here in Ireland. In many parts of the country, it was a 'Set Night' when a special tea was prepared with lots of hot potato cakes, gingerbread and apple tart – perhaps scattered through with the last of the mincemeat. But in other parts of the country, and in Munster in particular, it is better known as Nollaig na mBan, or Women's Christmas. This is definitely not a day for any woman to be slaving over a hot stove – unless of course you do as some ICA women do, and take it in turns to invite your women friends for an annual get-together.

New Year's Eve is another night that is associated with many different traditions in different parts of the country. For many people, it was traditionally a night for a simple tea, while for others it was the night to cook a goose – or two, depending on how much company you had. For much of the country, however, New Year's Eve was not a night to be indoors but rather one for gathering about a bonfire with friends and neighbours, seeing out the old year and welcoming the new one in.

In the New Year, may your right hand always be stretched out in friendship and never in want.

– Anonymous

THE NEW YEAR IN

"On New Year's Eve, my mam would make a big white soda bread which took centre place on the table for our tea at six o'clock. When we were all seated around the table, she would take the bread, go to the front door and tap the door with the bread. While she was doing this action she would recite a few times: 'The New Year in. The Old Year out, Trouble keep out, With each blessed day.' She would then cut the bread, which we all enjoyed."

– Kathleen Tessyman, Bantry Guild, Cork

"On New Year's Eve, householders in Cahersiveen, County Kerry would light a bonfire in the yard and all the family and visitors would stand around it raking the ashes saying goodbye to the old year and making wishes to welcome in the New Year.

My grandmother would bake an extra cake of bread on New Year's Day and put it outside on the windowsill overnight to ensure that hunger wouldn't cross the door during the year. The bread would be cut up the next day and given to the hens, cat and dog so they too wouldn't go hungry.

In Portmagee, County Kerry, people dressed up in fancy dress and masks. They walked through the village before midnight chasing a man in tattered clothes who represented 'the old year'. When he disappeared into the night they returned to welcome in the New Year with music, song and bonfires.

In many places it was considered bad luck if a red-haired woman was the first to enter your home on New Year's Day. In some parts of the country people wouldn't eat chicken on New Year's Day, the thinking being that as the chicken scratched behind her she would leave all the good luck behind her in the old year. Instead they would eat bacon or pork, because the pig scratches in front of him, to bring good luck for the coming year."

– Mary Curley, Lucan Guild, Dublin

Squash Soufflé

MARION LYON, MAGHERA GUILD, CAVAN

I believe vegetables are often overlooked in our Christmas menus. We in the Lyon family are big fans of squashes, having lived in the USA, where many different varies are available. This squash soufflé is ideal for the days after Christmas, when it will feed a gang, maybe with a crisp salad or some wilted greens on the side.

Serves 8–10

- 2 butternut squash
- 1–2 tablespoons rapeseed or olive oil
- 75g (2½oz) butter
- 2 tablespoons brown sugar
- ⅛ teaspoon salt
- ½ teaspoon finely grated orange zest
- ½ teaspoon ground nutmeg
- pinch of pepper
- 4 egg yolks
- 4 egg whites

To serve

- crisp salad or wilted greens

You'll also need

- 1 large soufflé dish, about 1½ litres (2½ pints)

1. Preheat oven to 200°C/400°F/Gas 6.
2. Trim the top and base from each squash, then stand them upright and halve lengthways. Scoop out the seeds, brush the exposed flesh with oil and roast flesh-side down in the preheated oven for 50–60 minutes or until the flesh is tender.
3. Remove the squash and reduce heat to 180°C/350°F/Gas 4.
4. Scoop out the cooked flesh into a large mixing bowl and combine with the butter, brown sugar, salt, orange zest, nutmeg and pepper. Add the egg yolks and beat well. Beat the egg whites stiffly and fold into the mixture.
5. Carefully fold the mixture into a large soufflé dish and bake in the preheated oven until set, about 55–60 minutes.

ICA Tip

A butternut squash will keep in a cool dark cupboard or larder for many weeks, so it's a good thing to have tucked away in case you need to whip something together when you've worked your way through the leftovers and the fridge is starting to look a little bare.

FROM 'THE JOURNEY OF THE MAGI'

'A cold coming we had of it,
Just the worst time of the year
For a journey, and such a long journey:
The ways deep and the weather sharp,
The very dead of winter.'
And the camels galled, sorefooted, refractory,
Lying down in the melting snow.
There were times we regretted
The summer palaces on slopes, the terraces,
And the silken girls bringing sherbet ...
A hard time we had of it ...

– T.S. Eliot

What would have happened if the Three Wise Men had been Three Wise Women?
They would have asked the way.
They would have arrived on time.
They would have delivered the baby.
They would have made a casserole.
They would have brought sensible gifts.
There would be Peace on Earth.

– Author unknown

" PS *If they were Derryquay women, they would have made a patchwork quilt.* "
– Celia Cooke, Derryquay Guild, Kerry

Portuguese Kings' Cake

JUNE FRADE LAWLESS, SHANKILL GUILD, DUBLIN

Various versions of this seasonal cake are eaten all over Europe at Christmas time, from Scandinavia to as far south as Portugal, where this recipe is from (as am I). Its name refers to the feast of the Three Kings, or the Feast of Epiphany, which is also known as Little Christmas here in Ireland.

Makes 1 loaf

- 1kg (2.2lb) strong flour
- 250g (9oz) sugar
- pinch of salt
- 6 eggs
- 6 egg yolks
- 300g (10½oz) butter, melted
- 200ml (7fl oz) milk, more if needed
- 150g (5½oz) raisins
- 100g (3½oz) orange and lemon peel
- 100g (3½oz) almonds
- 150g (5½oz) walnuts, broken into small pieces
- 50g (2oz) pine nuts

For the yeast starter

- 250g (9oz) strong flour
- 50g (2oz) yeast or a sachet of dried yeast
- 100ml (3½fl oz) milk

To finish

- crystallised fruit (pear, figs, orange, angelica, etc.)
- nuts (almonds, pine nuts, walnuts)
- caster sugar
- 1 egg, beaten with a little milk or water

You'll also need

- baking tray

1. To make the yeast starter, sieve the strong flour into a large mixing bowl, add the yeast and gradually add 100ml (3½fl oz) milk to bring it together into a dough. Cover the bowl with a tea towel and leave it somewhere warm overnight, or for at least 20 minutes, until doubled in size.

2. To make the bread dough, sieve the flour into another large mixing bowl, add the sugar and salt and mix to integrate. Make a well in the centre and transfer the starter into the centre.

3. In a separate bowl, beat the eggs and egg yolks together with the melted butter and milk and mix well to integrate. Gradually add this liquid to the mixing bowl, and bring it together to form a dough.

4. Knead well until you achieve the consistency of a light dough, then add the dried fruit, peel and nuts. Incorporate all ingredients and leave to prove for up to two hours or until the dough has doubled in size.

5. Preheat oven to 200°C/400°F/Gas 6.

6. Dust a flat baking tray with flour. Form the dough into a ring, placing a small ovenproof bowl in the centre to keep the shape.

7. Decorate the top of the ring with crystallised fruits or nuts of your choice, sprinkle well with caster sugar and brush generously with egg wash to give the loaf a glazed finish.

8. Bake in the preheated oven for 15 minutes, then reduce the heat to 180°C/350°F/Gas 4, and continue baking for a further 40–60 minutes or until golden.

9. Transfer to a wire rack to cool.

FROM 'THE DEAD'

– Where is Gabriel? she cried. Where on earth is Gabriel? There's everyone waiting in there, stage to let, and nobody to carve the goose!

– Here I am, Aunt Kate! cried Gabriel, with sudden animation, ready to carve a flock of geese, if necessary.

A fat brown goose lay at one end of the table, and at the other end, on a bed of creased paper strewn with sprigs of parsley, lay a great ham, stripped of its outer skin and peppered over with crust crumbs, a neat paper frill round its shin, and beside this was a round of spiced beef. Between these rival ends ran parallel lines of side-dishes: two little minsters of jelly, red and yellow; a shallow dish full of blocks of blancmange and red jam, a large green leaf-shaped dish with a stalk-shaped handle, on which lay bunches of purple raisins and peeled almonds, a companion dish on which lay a solid rectangle of Smyrna figs, a dish of custard topped with grated nutmeg, a small bowl full of chocolates and sweets wrapped in gold and silver papers and a glass vase in which stood some tall celery stalks. In the centre of the table there stood, as sentries to a fruit-stand which upheld a pyramid of oranges and American apples, two squat old-fashioned decanters of cut glass, one containing port and the other dark sherry. On the closed square piano a pudding in a huge yellow dish lay in waiting, and behind it were three squads of bottles of stout and ale and minerals drawn up according to the colours of their uniforms, the first two black, with brown and red labels, the third and smallest squad white, with transverse green sashes.

Gabriel took his seat boldly at the head of the table and, having looked to the edge of the carver, plunged his fork firmly into the goose. He felt quite at ease now, for he was an expert carver and liked nothing better than to find himself at the head of a well-laden table.

– Miss Furlong, what shall I send you? he asked. A wing or a slice of the breast?

– Just a small slice of the breast.

– Miss Higgins, what for you?

– O, anything at all, Mr Conroy.

While Gabriel and Miss Daly exchanged plates of goose and plates of ham and spiced beef, Lily went from guest to guest with a dish of hot floury potatoes wrapped in a white napkin. This was Mary Jane's idea and she had also suggested apple sauce for the goose, but Aunt Kate had said that plain roast goose without any apple sauce had always been good enough for her and she hoped she might never eat worse.

– James Joyce

Roast Goose with Apple Sauce

ELIZABETH MURPHY, BALLYROAN GUILD, LAOIS

Every year our family gave a turkey to a neighbour for Christmas and they gave us a goose for Little Christmas. We loved to serve the goose with a traditional potato stuffing and apple sauce.

Serves 6–8

- 4.5–5.5kg (10–12lb) goose, giblets removed and reserved
- salt
- ½ lemon
- 900g (2lb) potato stuffing, approximately (see page 149)

For the apple sauce

- 225g (½lb) cooking apples
- 2 tablespoons water
- 1 teaspoon caster sugar
- 15g (½oz) butter
- 1 teaspoon lemon juice

To serve

- roast potatoes (see page 151)
- giblet gravy (see page 148)

ICA Tip

Unlike turkey, the goose breast doesn't require basting, but you may wish to moisten the legs with some of the surplus fat about halfway through the cooking time, and to cover in foil to prevent burning.

1. Preheat oven to 170°C/325°F/Gas 3.

2. Singe any down or small feathers from the bird and prick the skin well with a sharp fork to allow excess fat to run off. Rub inside with salt and the cut side of the lemon half.

3. Stuff the cavity with potato stuffing and place breast-down on a rack in a roasting tin. Roast in the preheated oven for 3–3½ hours, depending on the size. (As goose is more similar to duck than it is to chicken or turkey, it can be served medium rare or pink. Over-cooked goose can taste 'livery'.)

4. Halfway through the roasting, turn the goose breast-side up and strain off the surplus fat from the baking tray through a sieve. Set this aside to cook your roast potatoes. (Any excess fat can be transferred to sterilised jam jars and stored in the fridge where it will keep well for up to six months.)

5. Meanwhile, make your giblet stock (see page 148) and apple sauce. Peel, core and chop or slice the apples. Simmer with the water until pulpy, then beat until smooth, adding the sugar, butter and lemon juice to taste. (If you prefer, you can cook the apples with a little water in a microwave, before adding the sugar, lemon juice and butter.) Set aside until ready to use.

6. Remove the goose from the roasting tin, cover in foil and set aside somewhere warm to rest for 30 minutes. Strain off the remaining fat from the roasting tin, leaving about two tablespoons in the baking tray, along with the sticky pan scrapings, which you'll want for the gravy.

7. Meanwhile, increase the oven heat to roast the potatoes (see page 151 or page 153) and prepare the giblet gravy (see page 148).

8. Before serving, heat through the apple sauce. Carve the goose breast and serve with the roast potatoes, apple sauce and giblet gravy.

THE FEAST OF EPIPHANY

"Epiphany is celebrated by Christians around the world on 6 January, marking the visit of the three wise men bringing gifts of gold, frankincense and myrrh. I read that there was an old Irish belief that when Christmas came to an end at midnight on 6 January, well water briefly turned to wine, rushes turned to silk and sandstone turned to gold!

In Ireland 6 January is also called Nollaig na mBan *or* Women's Christmas. *Traditionally this was the day when women got together and had their own 'Little Christmas' free from all the household jobs which allegedly were taken over by the men for the day.*

The UCC historian Alan Titley tells us that the earnings made by the women who reared a few turkeys for Christmas would have been used to buy the extra things for Christmas for the family and that they spent any leftover cash on themselves on Nollaig na mBan.
According to Bríd Mahon's book Land of Milk and Honey: The Story of Irish Traditional Food and Drink, *'High tea on the 6th January might have featured thinly cut sandwiches, scones, gingerbread, apple cakes, sponge cakes decorated with swirls of icing, plum cake, brown bread, soda bread, baker's bread, pats of freshly made butter, bowls of cream, dishes of jam and preserves and the best quality tea.'*

The Nollaig na mBan *tradition of women getting together is still very strong in Cork. I found this out some years ago when staying with friends in Cork. We happily set out from Crosshaven into the city to have a meal. It was a* Monday *night so we hadn't thought it was necessary to book. Every single restaurant was full and there wasn't a man to be seen in any of them! We headed back out to find the same situation in Carrigaline and Crosshaven.*

In the past respectable women would not go into a pub except perhaps for a glass of stout during the day when they were in town shopping, as it was believed that stout was a good way of getting iron. But my Cork relatives tell me that on the night of Nollaig na mBan *women would gather in the snug of a bar and drink stout and eat thick corned beef sandwiches.*

The Nollaig na mBan *tradition of women getting together has perhaps died out in parts of the country, but it is being revived in other parts. Now groups of women gather in restaurants and hotels and comfortable lounges for high-end meals, and the bottle of wine has replaced the bottle of stout.*

In Ashford Guild we have celebrated Nollaig na mBan *every year since 1992 with a meal out, or a trip to the concert hall or theatre. It's a great tradition.* Go maire sé i bhfad."

– Hilda Roche, Ashford Guild, Wicklow

Spiced Beef

ANNE HARRINGTON, BLACKROCK GUILD, DUBLIN

My husband's Aunt Nancy first introduced me to this Munster dish, along with the tradition of celebrating Nollaig na mBan at Little Christmas. I like to serve it with apricot and almond chutney (see page 58), as inspired by the Bord Bia website. You can buy some excellent spiced beef – certain butchers in Cork are particularly famous for theirs – but it's nice to make it yourself.

Serves 10

- 5kg (6½lb) beef – topside or silverside works well, as does flank
- 75g (2½oz) brown sugar
- 25g (1oz) black peppercorns
- 25g juniper berries
- 12g allspice berries
- 15g (½oz) ground cloves
- 15g (½oz) salt
- 15g (½oz) saltpetre (available from chemists)

To serve

- brown bread (see page 21)
- apricot and almond chutney (see page 58)

1. Trim the beef of any excess fat and gristle, if any. Rub the beef all over with the sugar, cover and leave for 2 days in a bowl in the fridge.

2. Crush the peppercorns, juniper and allspice berries together in a mortar and pestle. Mix with the cloves, salt and saltpetre. Rub the beef thoroughly with the spice mixture.

3. Re-cover and store in the fridge for a week, turning daily to ensure an even spicing.

4. To cook the beef, preheat oven to 140°C/275°F/Gas 1. Place the beef in a deep casserole with a tightly fitting lid. Add 275ml (½ pint) water and cover tightly.

5. Cook in the preheated oven for 5 hours. Allow the beef to cool in the liquid for 2–3 hours.

6. Wrap the beef in tinfoil and store in the fridge until ready to serve. Serve thinly sliced on brown bread with apricot and almond chutney.

FROM 'WINTERTIME'

Little Christmas is over once more
And the festive lights are gone.
It's back to the dreary and drab old hues
That we've had since the sun last shone.
Still, days are getting longer now
And soon things will be back to normal ...

– Connie McEvoy, Termonfeckin Guild, Louth

Deep peace of the running wave to you,
Deep peace of the flowing air to you,
Deep peace of the quiet earth to you,
Deep peace of the shining stars to you,
Deep peace of the Son of Peace to you.

– Celtic blessing

O after Christmas we'll have no need to go searching
For the difference that sets an old phrase burning –
We'll hear it in the whispered argument of a churning
Or in the streets where the village boys are lurching.
And we'll hear it among decent men too
Who barrow dung in gardens under trees,
Wherever life pours ordinary plenty ...

– Patrick Kavanagh, from 'Advent'

Appendices

Acknowledgements
Useful Equipment & Glossary
Contributors

Acknowledgements

As with all our books, this unique and special book would not have been possible without the work of the ICA members. I would like to take this opportunity to thank each of the members who sent in their submissions. Some of those received do not appear in this book, but all of them are treasured, and each submission has helped to influence and shape the book. A special word of thanks to Josephine Helly for casting her expert eye over the crafts element if this book.

I would like to thank Liz Wall for her work on overseeing the publication of this book at the end of her three-year term as National President, as well as Rebecca Ryan and Colette Downing for their help in co-ordinating the extensive submissions.

I would also like to thank our wonderful editor Aoife Carrigy and all at our publishers, Gill & Macmillan, as well as the team who worked so effectively to make this another handsome publication of which we can be proud: stylists Carly Horan and Blondie Horan, photographer Joanne Murphy and designer Tanya Ross.

Marie O'Toole, National President of the Irish Countrywomen's Association

Useful Equipment & Glossary

A FEW WORDS ABOUT TEMPERATURES AND MEASUREMENTS

Note that, unless otherwise specified, temperatures given throughout this book are for conventional ovens. If you have a fan oven, reduce the suggested temperature by about 20°C (e.g. from 200°C to 180°C).

Note that tablespoon measurements are for a full-sized tablespoon, which is larger than a dessertspoon. All teaspoon measurements are for a level teaspoon, unless otherwise specified.

Both metric and imperial measurements have been provided. It is best to follow one or the other, as in some cases they have been rounded up or down (1oz = 28g, not 25g) for practicality.

Useful Equipment

Baking parchment: also known as silicone paper, baking paper or greaseproof paper, this is essential for many baking recipes in order to line the tins; it's also useful for sealing jars of homemade preserves or mincemeat.

Baking sheet: a flat baking sheet (as opposed to a shallow baking tray) is very useful for baking certain breads and cakes, and can be preheated for optimum results.

Blender: a stand-alone electrical appliance used for chopping, mixing or liquidising foods.

Bun tin: also known as a patty tin, this is a baking tray with six, nine or 12 cup depressions for making buns and mini pies.

Cake tin: cake tins come in various sizes and shapes. If you are using a square tin rather than a round one, reduce the dimensions by 2½ cm (1in).

Casserole: a large ovenproof lidded dish for cooking large stews in the oven or on the stovetop.

Chopping board: it is good practice to allocate one chopping board to dealing with raw meats and fish, another for vegetables including pungent onions and garlic, and another for fruits and bread. Always wash your chopping board in hot soapy water after dealing with raw meat and fish.

Cook's knife: a good, well-maintained knife will do much to improve your cooking; always store it carefully to keep it as sharp as possible and sharpen it regularly.

Delph bowl: a traditional delph or ceramic mixing bowl can useful for soaking or marinating ingredients because it is less likely than plastic to absorb odours.

Flan tin: also known as a quiche tin or tart tin, these often have a removable base.

Food processor: a multi-functional appliance that has a container and a number of different removable revolving blades, which allows food to be cut, sliced, shredded, blended, beaten or liquidised in the container.

Frying pan: whether you have a modern non-stick frying pan or an old-fashioned cast iron one, the weight of the pan is important; a heavy-based pan will distribute heat more evenly and be less likely to burn food.

Grater: a good grater is a real friend in the kitchen; look for one with several grades of fineness or invest in a selection of quality graters.

Hand blender: also known as a billy, a hand-held electrical appliance is useful for liquidising, blending or puréeing foods such as soups without transferring them from the cooking vessel.

Labels: a roll of labels is an essential piece of kitchen kit if you plan to do any freezing or preserving, in order to record exactly what you made and when.

Loaf tin: tins for bread making are usually defined by the volume they hold rather than their shape (e.g. a 900g/2lb loaf tin).

Measuring jug: plastic, Pyrex or glass jug for measuring liquids. It is worth having one that gives metric and imperial measurements as well as American cups.

Measuring spoons: collection of stainless steel spoons, including teaspoons and tablespoons; useful to have for baking as many households no longer have a full-sized tablespoon in their cutlery set.

Melon baller: useful for balling melon or potatoes and for coring apples and pears.

Mixer: a stand-alone electrical appliance with interchangeable blades; useful for everything from folding and whipping to beating and mixing ingredients.

Palette knife: useful for smoothing surfaces such as icing and for loosening and lifting cakes from baking tins.

Pastry brush: useful for glazing pastries as well as other jobs such as basting; a silicone brush is easier to wash than a traditional brush, but tends to retain less liquid.

Pastry cutter: also known as scone cutter or cookie cutter; it is useful to have a variety of sizes for use in all sorts of baking.

Peeler: life is too short to use a bad peeler; there are various versions out there so experiment and when you find one that works for you, hold on to it.

Pestle and mortar: granite, ceramic or wooden bowl (mortar) with accompanying hand-held utensil for grinding or crushing ingredients.

Piping bag: handy for decorating cakes with precision.

Ramekin: individual round ceramic dishes useful for making various pies and puddings.

Roasting rack: also known as a trivet, this is a little metal stand on which you can sit ingredients in a roasting tin so that they do not touch the base of the tin; useful for roasting fatty poultry such as duck or goose.

Rolling pin: a good rolling pin is essential for baking with pastry; some people like to use a ceramic or marble one to keep pastry extra cool.

Sieve: it is worth having a general sieve for use with dry ingredients when baking as well as a colander (for draining wet ingredients) and perhaps a fine chinois for passing purées.

Skewers: a metal skewer is very useful for judging whether food is cooked, from meats and fish to cakes and baking.

Slow cooker: also known as a crockpot, this stand-alone appliance is ideal for very slow unsupervised cooking.

Spatula: a rubber 'spoon' spatula is useful in baking; it's handy for scraping down and incorporating ingredients that have stuck to the sides of a mixing bowl, as well as for smoothing a cake mixture into the baking tin. You may also need a separate flat frosting spatula or palette knife for icing cakes.

Spring-form tin: baking tin with adjustable sides that allow the tin to be easily removed.

Thermometer: a sugar or jam thermometer may be worth investing in if you plan on making a lot of jam. A meat thermometer is useful to judge the central temperature of a large joint of meat.

Twine: essential for the traditional wrapping and sealing of Christmas puddings before steaming.

Waxed discs: these are useful for sealing homemade preserves and are readily available in kitchen shops or online; alternatively, you can cut your own from baking parchment.

Weighing scales: if you like to bake, electronic scales might be worth investing in, as they allow you to measure weights very precisely.

Wire rack: cooling rack for use in baking; the circulation of air is essential for forming a good crust on bread and to allow cakes to cool evenly.

Glossary

Basting: periodically moistening roasting meat with its cooking juices.

Bextartar: a make of cream of tartar.

Bicarbonate of soda: also known as sodium bicarbonate, bread soda or baking soda, this is different from baking powder; it requires an acid such as buttermilk or cream of tartar to activate its leavening properties.

Bind: to moisten and bring together dry ingredients with a small amount of liquid in order to form into a paste or dough.

Blanch: a technique of par-cooking vegetables, involving boiling them briefly before arresting the cooking in cold or iced water to retain a firm texture and bright colour. Shelled nuts such as almonds are blanched (soaked in boiling water) to loosen the skin before removing it.

Blitz: to blend to a purée with a hand blender or in a blender.

Creaming: blending butter and sugar until light and fluffy and about doubled in volume; this is traditionally achieved by beating with a wooden spoon, but using an electric beater is more convenient.

Cream of tartar: a raising agent generally used for making soda bread, when it is combined with regular milk in place of buttermilk or sour milk.

Crimp: a term for impressing a patterned seal on a pastry rim; this can be done with fingers, a fork or a knife.

Descale: to remove the scales from the skin of fish; this can be a messy business, so ask your fishmonger to do it if he hasn't already.

Fold: in baking, the gentle action of folding incorporates dry ingredients such as flour or sugar into whipped ingredients such as whipped egg white or cream while retaining as much air as possible in the whipped ingredients.

Fillet: if buying whole fish, you can ask your fishmonger to prepare it by gutting it and removing the head and bones.

Pin-boning: some fillets of fish will still have large pin-bones running down along the side of the fillet; check for these with your fingers and remove with a pair of large flat tweezers.

Sauté: to fry vegetables such as onion very quickly in order to brown and caramelise them while cooking; do not stir too often.

Searing: also known as browning; to cook meat quickly on a high heat in order to encourage the sugars to caramelise.

Sweat: to fry vegetables such as onion very slowly and gently in order to soften them without browning; it helps to cover with a lid and perhaps some greaseproof paper to keep the moisture in.

Toast: nuts, seeds and spices can be toasted on a dry frying pan, under a hot grill or in a low oven in order to release aromas; watch closely to catch them before they burn.

Contributors

The ICA would like to thank all the Guilds and individual members who shared their memories of Christmases past, tried and tested recipes and treasured lines from seasonal prose and poetry to help us compile this special festive book.

Ada Vance, Killeshandra Guild, Cavan
Aloma McKay, Ennistymon Guild, Clare
Anne Harrington, Blackrock Guild, Dublin
Anne O'Connor, Oulart Guild, Wexford
Anne Payne, Portlaoise Guild, Laois
Anne Maria Dennison, Mainistir na Féile Guild, Limerick
Audrey Starrett, Raphoe Guild, Donegal
Betty Gorman, Castletown Guild, Laois
Breda Murray, Ardmore Grange Guild, Waterford
Brenda Leary, Blackrock Guild, Louth
Breda O'Donnell, Scariff Guild, Clare
Breege Quinn, Ennybegs Guild, Longford
Bridgid Keane, Ardmore Grange Guild, Waterford
Bridie Lyne, Annascaul Guild, Kerry
Bridie O'Shea, Mainistir Na Féile Guild, Limerick
Brigid O'Brien, Aughadown Guild, Cork
Brona Ui Loing, Kilteel Guild, Kildare
Caroline Flynn, Castleknock Guild, Dublin
Caroline Power, Ratoath Guild, Meath
Catherine Charles, Aughavas Guild, Leitrim
Catherine Gallagher, Newtowncashel Guild, Longford
Catherine Murphy, Caherdavin Guild, Limerick
Celia Cooke, Derryquay Guild, Kerry
Claire Ann McDonnell, Moneystown Guild, Wicklow
Christina McKenna, Scariff Guild, Clare
Connie McEvoy, Termonfeckin Guild, Louth
Debra Dunne, Swords Guild, Dublin
Deirdre Connery, Duncannon Guild, Wexford
Dora Kennedy, Annascaul Guild, Kerry
Eileen Pollock, Marshes Guild, Louth
Eilish McDonnell, Horseleap Streamstown Guild, Westmeath
Eily Kennedy, Annascaul Guild, Kerry
Elaine Hynes, Castlebar Guild, Mayo
Eleanor Carleton, Clones Guild, Monaghan
Elizabeth Murphy, Ballyroan Guild, Laois
Geraldine O'Connor, Clones Guild, Monaghan
Gerardine Rogers, Scariff Guild, Clare
Heather Evans, Clonakenny Guild, Tipperary
Helen Faughnan, Mohill Guild, Leitrim
Helen Kavanagh, Borris-in-Ossory Guild, Laois
Helen O'Shea, Newtowncashel Guild, Longford
Helen Weir, Two Mile House Guild, Kildare
Hilda Roche, Ashford Guild, Wicklow
Imelda Byrne, Leighlinbridge Guild, Carlow
Irene O'Brien, Scotshouse Guild, Monaghan
Jackie Slattery, Clooney Quin Guild, Clare
Jane Johnston, Longford Town Guild, Longford
Janet Murphy, Clochan/Bhreanainn Guild, Kerry
Joan Connelly, Templemore Guild, Tipperary
Joan Hayes, Crecora Guild, Limerick
JoAnn Lenehan, Annascaul Guild, Kerry

Joe (Josephine) Keane, Wexford Town Guild, Wexford
Josie Kenny, Aughavas Guild, Leitrim
Julia Carty (RIP), Moore Guild, Roscommon
Julie Marshall, Cloone Guild, Leitrim
June Frade Lawless, Shankill Guild, Dublin
Karen Ryan, Wexford Town Guild, Wexford
Kathleen Leahy, Mainistir na Féile Guild, Limerick
Kathleen O'Connor, Broadford Guild, Limerick
Kathleen Tessyman, Bantry Guild, Cork
Kathy Le Brasse, Drogheda Guild, Louth
Kay Devine, Bonniconlon Guild, Mayo
Kay Murray, Broadford Guild, Clare
Lily McDonald, Ballyroan Guild, Laois
Liz O'Leary, Annascaul Guild, Kerry
Liz Wall, Ashford Guild, Wicklow
Louie Taylor, Finn Valley Guild, Donegal
Mai Kelly, Moydow Guild, Longford
Mairead O'Gorman, Camross Guild, Wexford
Máire Treanor, Clones Guild, Monaghan
Mamo McDonald, Clones Guild, Monaghan
Margaret Cunningham, Coolaney Guild, Sligo
Margaret Kyne Doyle, Knocknacarra Guild, Galway
Margaret McDonald, Legan Guild, Longford
Margaret Dodo McKenna, Clones Guild, Monaghan
Marian Cole, Drogheda Guild, Louth
Marian Lawless, Portlaoise Guild, Laois
Marie Henry, Behy Guild, Mayo
Marion Ferguson, Clones Guild, Monaghan
Marion Lyon, Maghera Guild, Cavan
Mary Birney, Minaun Guild, Waterford
Mary Carton, Suncroft Guild, Kildare
Mary Curley, Lucan Guild, Dublin
Mary Duffy, Liffey Valley Guild, Dublin
Mary Dunbar, Lakeview Guild, Sligo
Mary Gavin, Clifden Guild, Galway
Mary Haran, Coolaney Guild, Sligo
Mary Harkin, Lakeview Guild, Sligo
Mary McCarthy, Rathkeevan Guild, Tipperary
Mary MacNamara, Maynooth Guild, Kildare
Mary MacRedmond, Clara Guild, Offaly
Mary O'Gorman, Maynooth Guild, Kildare
Mary Sherry, Ballinode Guild, Monaghan
Mary Spillane, Derryquay Guild, Kerry
Mary White, Barna Guild, Galway
Maura Kenny, Moore Guild, Roscommon
Maura Riordan, Dun Laoghaire Guild, Dublin
Mella Winters, Taghmon Guild, Wexford
Miriam Murphy, Blanchardstown Guild, Dublin
Niamh Headon, Ballymore Eustace Guild, Kildare
Patricia Carbin, Ballinode Guild, Monaghan
Patricia Cavanagh, Ballinode Guild, Monaghan
Patricia O'Toole, Newbridge Guild, Kildare Federation
Pauline Bligh, Lucan Guild, Dublin
Peg Prendeville, Ballyhahill/Loughill Guild, Limerick
Peggy Curran, Clones Guild, Monaghan
Peggy Lynch, Drumshanbo Guild, Leitrim
Peggy Ryan Luke, Cappamore Guild, Limerick
Rose Connolly, Drombanna Guild, Limerick
Rosemary Carleton, Clones Guild, Monaghan
Rosemary McCarville, Clones Guild, Monaghan
Stephanie Igoe, Ennybegs Guild, Longford
Susan Potts, Drogheda Guild, Louth
Vivienne McGirr, Raphoe Guild, Donegal
Winnie McCarron, Ballinode Guild, Monaghan

Index

A

B

C

D

E

F

G